101 Stocking Stuffers

Oxmoor House®

101 Stocking Stuffers

Published by Oxmoor House, Inc., Leisure Arts, Inc., and Symbol of Excellence Publishers, Inc.

Library of Congress Catalog Number: 93-87578
Hardcover ISBN: 0-8487-1173-4
Softcover ISBN: 0-8487-1420-2
Manufactured in the United States of America
First Printing 1994

Oxmoor House, Inc.
Editor-in-Chief: Nancy J. Fitzpatrick
Senior Editor: Mary Kay Culpepper
Editor: Cecilia C. Robinson
Copy Editor: Susan Smith Cheatham
Copy Assistant: Leslee Rester Johnson
Production Manager: Rick Litton
Associate Production Manager: Theresa L. Beste
Production Assistant: Marianne Jordan

PJS Publications, Inc.
Book Editor: Carol Zentgraf

Symbol of Excellence Publishers, Inc.
Editors: Barbara Cockerham, Phyllis Hoffman
Editorial Assistants: Susan Branch, Carol Odom
Production Manager: Wayne Hoffman
Associate Production Manager: Perry James
Creative Director: Mac Jamieson
Executive Art Director: Yukie McLean
Graphic Designers: Dottie Barton, Scott Begley,
    Michael Whisenant
Illustrator: Laurie Baker
Photographer: David L. Maxwell
Photography Stylists: Cathy Muir, Angela Stiff,
    Jarinda Wiechman

Introduction

Hanging the stockings "by the chimney with care" as the well-known poem by Clement C. Moore goes, is a time-honored holiday tradition. Of all the Christmas memories, the one we best recall with that long-ago child's sense of wonder is the Christmas Eve tradition of hanging our stockings in anticipation of Santa's annual visit. It mattered not whether we had a fireplace with a mantel or, for lack of a mantel, a doorknob or chair took its place. Santa always found those stockings, and we were always delighted come Christmas morn.

We've decided that Santa, having spent years of holidays distributing toys and gifts, might welcome some assistance. So we put on our warm knitted thinking caps and came up with a magical array of 101 stocking stuffers that you can make for this season. We think you will agree that this exciting collection has something for everyone—great ideas for cousins, granny and grandpa, and friends who would treasure a handcrafted gift.

Of course not all the gifts we have selected will fit in an ordinary stocking. But the ideas were so clever that we couldn't resist sharing them with you. So choose your favorites and get set for hours of crafting fun as you make tomorrow's memories.

Happy holidays!

Contents

Quick & Easy Accessories

For Tots to Teens

Fun Kids' Crafts

Stockings to Stuff

Everyone needs a stocking at Christmastime. This collection of festive "footwear," intended especially for holding treats and treasures, will inspire you to create a favorite for every member of your family including the dog and cat!

Whether you choose the elegant and richly colored Victorian crazy-quilt stocking, the traditional red-and-green knitted version, or a cross-stitched beauty, you'll feel a sense of personal satisfaction December 24th when your loved ones gather to hang their stockings in anticipation of Christmas morn.

We have chosen stockings that represent several disciplines: knitting, crochet, yo-yo quilting, appliqué, crazy quilting, cross stitch, and craft painting. From quick-to-complete cross stitch worked on the cuffs of purchased stockings to a glamorously painted design, eleven wonderful stockings await you!

Victorian Patchwork Stocking

Materials:
½ yd. 44/45"-wide teal taffeta (for stocking)
½ yd. 44/45"-wide burgundy taffeta (for lining)
6"-square scraps of laces and fabrics in coordinating colors (for patchwork)
18" square cotton batiste fabric (for patchwork foundation)
½ yd. fleece
1½ yds. St. Louis Trimming ¾"-wide antique gold metallic lace
6" length St. Louis Trimming ½"-wide antique gold metallic lace (for hanger)
2 yds. 1½"-wide burgundy wired ribbon (for bow)
1 yd. narrow piping cord
Assorted gold charms, buttons, ribbon roses
Sewing machine
Threads to match fabrics
Iron
Tracing paper
Scissors

Note: Unless otherwise indicated, all seam allowances are ¼" and all seams are sewn with right sides facing.

1. Enlarge patterns as indicated. Trace patterns onto tracing paper, adding ¼" seam allowance, and cut out.
2. Cut pieces from fabric and fleece as indicated on patterns. Cut one 1" x 36" bias strip from teal taffeta to cover piping cord.
3. Cover each batiste foundation piece with crazy quilt patchwork, following instructions on page **49**. Trim patchwork even with foundation edges.
4. Baste one fleece piece to the wrong side of each teal stocking piece. Baste patchwork heel and toe pieces to the right side of one stocking piece, aligning edges. Topstitch ¾"-wide metallic lace along inside curved edge of heel and toe pieces. Cover piping cord with taffeta bias strip. Aligning raw edges, sew covered piping to side and bottom edges of stocking front. Sew stocking front and back together, leaving top edge open. Trim seam, clip curves, and turn.

5. Fold patchwork cuff piece in half; sew short edges together. Repeat for taffeta cuff lining piece. Align seams and sew patchwork cuff and lining pieces together along scalloped edge. Trim seam, turn, and press. Topstitch ¾"-wide metallic lace along scalloped edge. Baste top edges of cuff together and sew to top of stocking, aligning top edges and seams. Make a loop with ½"-wide metallic braid. Sew to back seam of cuff, with raw edges of loop at cuff top.
6. Sew burgundy stocking lining pieces together, leaving top edge open and a 3" opening in the bottom for turning; do not turn. Clip curves. Place stocking inside lining with right sides facing and seams aligned. Sew together along top edges. Pull stocking through opening in bottom of lining. Slipstitch opening closed and insert lining in stocking.
7. Referring to photo, sew charms and ribbon roses to patchwork pieces. Make a multi-loop bow with wired burgundy ribbon and sew to top back edge of stocking front.

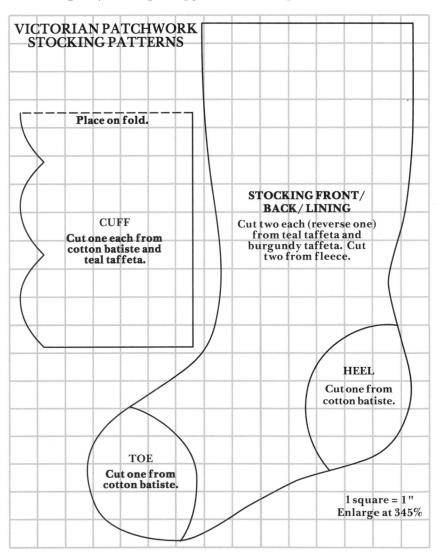

VICTORIAN PATCHWORK STOCKING PATTERNS

Place on fold.

CUFF
Cut one each from cotton batiste and teal taffeta.

STOCKING FRONT/ BACK/LINING
Cut two each (reverse one) from teal taffeta and burgundy taffeta. Cut two from fleece.

HEEL
Cut one from cotton batiste.

TOE
Cut one from cotton batiste.

1 square = 1"
Enlarge at 345%

Kitten & Puppy Stockings

Stockings for Pets

Kitten & Puppy Stockings

DMC	Color
● 310	black
⊂ 321	red
▲ 909	emerald, vy. dk.
\ white	white

Fabric: 14-count white Aida cuff of Christmas Dot Stocking from Charles Craft, Inc.

Stitch count: 30H x 65W

Design size:
11-count 2¾" x 5⅞"
14-count 2⅛" x 4⅝"
18-count 1⅝" x 3⅝"
22-count 1⅜" x 3"

Instructions: Cross stitch using two strands of floss. Backstitch using one strand of 310. Center design on cross-stitch fabric cuff of stocking.

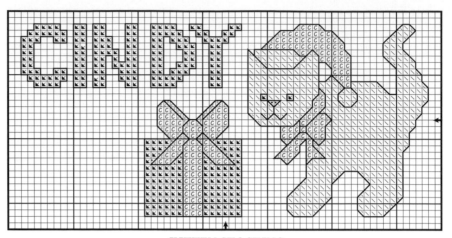

KITTEN STOCKING

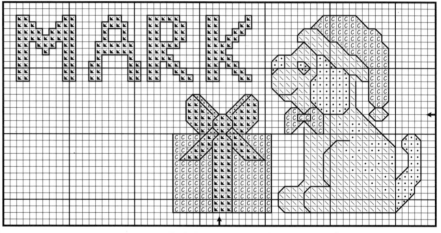

PUPPY STOCKING

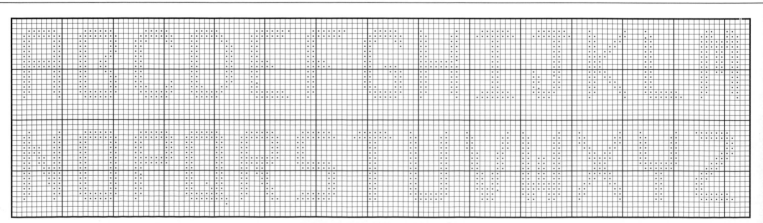

KITTEN & PUPPY STOCKINGS ALPHABET

DOG STOCKING ALPHABET

Stockings for Pets

	DMC	Color
•	white	white
X	321	red

Dog Stocking
Fabric: 14-count red Aida from Zweigart®

Cat Stocking
Fabric: 14-count white Aida from Zweigart®
Stitch count: 19H x 61W
Design size:
11-count 1¾" x 5⅝"
14-count 1⅜" x 4⅜"
18-count 1⅛" x 3⅜"
22-count ⅞" x 2¾"

Instructions: Chart letters for dog's name and cross stitch using three strands white. Cross stitch sentiment on cat stocking using two strands 321.

Dog Stocking
Materials:
½ yd. 44/45"-wide Christmas calico fabric
6" square red-and-white pindot fabric
8" square transfer fusing web
1 yd. red piping
4" length ⅜"-wide red satin ribbon
2 yds. ⅛"-wide red satin ribbon (cut into 10" lengths)
Green bone-shaped dog treats
Red and green sewing threads
Sewing machine
Glue gun (optional)
Tracing paper
Scissors
Iron

Note: Unless otherwise indicated, all seam allowances are ¼" and all seams are sewn with right sides facing.

1. Cross stitch dog's name following instructions given. With name centered, trim fabric to 2" x 6¼".
2. Enlarge patterns as indicated, trace onto tracing paper, and cut out. Cut pieces from fabric as indicated on patterns.
3. For stocking front, follow manufacturer's instructions for fusible webbing and fuse cross-stitched fabric 1" down from top

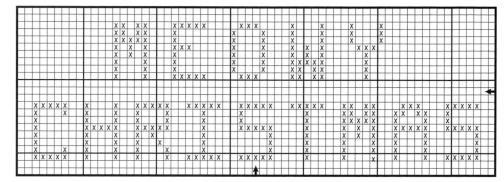

CAT STOCKING

DOG STOCKING PATTERN

STOCKING FRONT/BACK/LINING
Cut four (reverse two) from Christmas calico.

TOE
Cut one from pindot.

HEEL
Cut one from pindot.

Dots indicate ribbon placement.

1 square = 1"
Enlarge at 163%

edge on right side of one stocking piece. Fuse toe and heel pindot pieces in place. Machine satin-stitch edges of fused pieces using green thread.

4. Aligning raw edges, baste piping to side and bottom edges of stocking front. Sew stocking front and back together, leaving top edge open. Trim seam, clip curves, and turn. Fold ⅜"-wide ribbon in half to form a loop. Baste to top right corner of stocking, aligning raw edges of stocking and ribbon. For the lining, sew the two remaining stocking pieces together along side and bottom edges, leaving a 3" opening in bottom for turning; do not turn. Clip curves. Place stocking inside lining with right sides facing and back seams aligned. Sew together along top edges. Pull stocking through opening in lining and slipstitch opening closed. Insert lining in stocking and press.

5. Sew centers of ⅛"-wide ribbon lengths to stocking front as indicated by dots on pattern. Tie each ribbon into a bow around a dog treat.

Cat Stocking
Materials:
½ yd. 44/45"-wide blue fabric
8" square yellow print fabric
10" x 4" piece dark blue fabric
Fabric scraps: green pindot, red, gray
12" square transfer fusing web
1 yd. red piping
4" length ⅜"-wide red satin ribbon (for hanger)
8" length ⅛"-wide red satin ribbon
Embroidery floss, colors: pink, white, black
Three ⅜" gold heart buttons
Two ¼" round black buttons
10-mm green bell
Scraps of gold braid
Threads to match fabrics
Sewing machine
Tracing paper
Scissors   Iron

1. Cross stitch message following instructions given on page 13. With message centered, trim fabric to 2" x 6¼".

2. Enlarge patterns as indicated. Trace stocking pattern onto tracing paper and cut out. Cut from fabric as indicated on pattern. Trace appliqué patterns onto

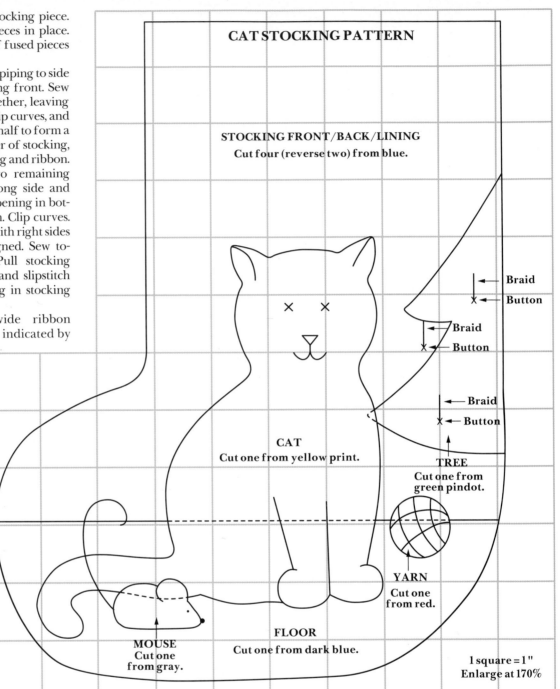

CAT STOCKING PATTERN

STOCKING FRONT/BACK/LINING
Cut four (reverse two) from blue.

←— Braid
←— Button

←— Braid
←— Button

←— Braid
←— Button

CAT
Cut one from yellow print.

TREE
Cut one from green pindot.

YARN
Cut one from red.

MOUSE
Cut one from gray.

FLOOR
Cut one from dark blue.

1 square = 1"
Enlarge at 170%

tracing paper and cut out. Reverse patterns and trace onto paper side of fusible webbing; cut apart between motifs. Follow manufacturer's instructions to fuse motifs to wrong side of fabrics as indicated on patterns. Cut out motifs on pattern lines and peel away paperbacking.

3. For stocking front, refer to photo for appliqué placement. Fuse cross-stitched fabric 1" down from top edge of one stocking piece. Fuse floor and tree, and then cat, mouse, and yarn in place. Machine satin-stitch edges of pieces and detail lines using green thread for Aida strip, white for cat, and matching threads for remaining

pieces. For cat, embroider nose with pink floss and mouth with white floss. Sew on black buttons for eyes and ⅛"-wide red ribbon for a collar. For mouse, make French knot with pink floss for nose and a French knot with black floss for eye. Cut three ½" lengths of braid and sew to tree as indicated on pattern. Sew gold button to bottom of each braid length.

4. Follow instructions for *Dog Stocking* to add piping and hanging loop and to assemble stocking and lining.

5. Tie remaining ⅛"-wide ribbon into a bow and tack to center of collar. Sew bell to collar under bow.

Crochet & Knit Stockings

Crochet Stocking

Length: 18"

Materials:
Unger Utopia (100-gr./240 yds. worsted-weight acrylic), 1 skein each ecru #111 (A), red #185 (B), and green #146 (C)
Size J/10 (6 mm) crochet hook or size to obtain gauge
Yarn needle

Gauge
15 sc = 4"
16 dc = 4"

Abbreviations
beg = beginning
ch(s) = chain(s)
dc = double crochet
dec = decrease
est = established
hdc = half double crochet
lp(s) = loop(s)
rem = remaining
rep = repeat
sc = single crochet
sk = skip
sl st = slip stitch
st(s) = stitch(es)
tr = treble crochet
yo = yarn over

Note: To change colors, work last yo of color being worked with next color.

Cuff
With A, ch 51.
Row 1: Sc in 2nd ch from hook and each in ch across; turn—50 sts.
Rows 2-17: Ch 1, sc in each sc across, working last yo of last sc on row 17 with B, turn.

Leg
Row 18: With B, ch 3 (counts as dc), sk first sc, dc in each st across; turn.
Row 19: Ch 3 (counts as dc), dc in each st across; turn.
Rows 20, 21: With C, ch 3 (counts as dc), dc in each st across; turn.
Rows 22-29: Rep rows 18-20, working in est color pattern. Work last yo of last dc on row 29 with A; turn.

Heel
First Half: Row 1: With A, ch 1, sc in first 13 dc; turn.
Rows 2-9: Ch 1, sc in 13 sc; turn.
Row 10: Ch 1, sc in 4 sc, draw up lp in next 2 sc, yo and draw through all lps on hook (sc dec made), sc in next sc; turn.
Row 11: Ch 1, sc in 6 sc; turn.
Row 12: Ch 1, sc in 6 sc, sc dec, sc in next sc; turn.
Row 13: Ch 1, sc in 8 sc; turn.
Row 14: Ch 1, sc in 8 sc, sc dec, sc in next sc; turn.
Row 15: Ch 1, sc in 10 sc; fasten off.
Second Half: Row 1: Attach A at opposite end of last row of Leg, ch 1, sc in first, 13 dc; turn.
Rows 2-15: Rep rows 2-15 as for first half of heel.

Foot
Row 1: Attach B at side edge of Heel, ch 3 (counts as dc), work 13 dc on edge of first half of heel, dc in each of center 24 dc of leg, work 13 dc on edge of 2nd half of heel; turn—50 dc.

Row 2: Ch 3 (counts as dc), dc in each st across; turn.
Rows 3, 4: With C, rep row 2.
Row 5: With B, rep row 2.
Row 6: With B, ch 3 (counts as dc), dc in next dc; * holding back last lp of each st on hook, dc in next 2 dc, yo and draw through all lps on hook (dc dec made), dc in 3 dc; rep from * across, end last rep with dc in 1 dc; turn—40 dc.
Rows 7-9: Rep row 2 in est color pattern.
Row 10: With B, ch 3 (counts as dc); * dc dec, dc in 2 dc; rep from * across, end last rep with dc in 1 dc; turn—30 dc.
Rows 11, 12: With C, rep row 2, working last yo of last dc on row 12 with A.

Toe
Rows 1-7: Ch 1, sc in each st across; turn.
Row 8: Ch 1, work sc dec across; turn—15 sc.
Row 9: Rep row 1; fasten off, leaving a tail.

Finishing
1. **Cross Stitching:** Following chart, center snowflake motifs in cuff.
2. Weave tail of yarn through rem sts on toe and pull tightly to close. Sew seam.
3. **Top Edging and Hanging Loop:**
Row 1: Attach C to top band at the back seam, ch 3, dc in each sc around; sl st with B to top of beg ch-3.
Row 2: Ch 4, work (dc, hdc, sc) in next dc; * sk 2 dc, sc in next dc, sk 2 dc, in next dc work (sc, hdc, dc, tr, dc, hdc, sc) for shell; rep from * across ending with half shell (sc, hdc, dc), sl st to top of beg ch-4; ch 15; sc in 2nd ch from hook and in each rem ch; fasten off.
Fold chain in half and attach end at base of ch.

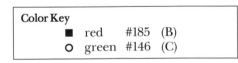

Color Key		
■ red	#185	(B)
O green	#146	(C)

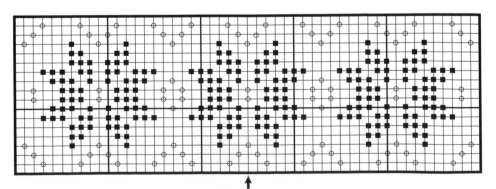

CROCHET STOCKING

Knit Stocking

Length: Approximately 17½"

Materials:
Reynolds Paterna (50-gr./110 yds. worsted-weight wool), 2 skeins ecru #30 (A); 1 skein each blue #315 (B), red #218 (C), and green #514 (D)
One pair size 7 (4.5 mm) needles or size to obtain gauge
Size E/4 (3.5 mm) crochet hook
Yarn needle   Two stitch holders

Gauge

In St st, 5 sts and 7 rows = 1"

Abbreviations

beg = beginning
ch = chain
CO = cast on
cont = continue
dec = decrease
est = established
K = knit
P = purl
rem = remaining
rep = repeat
RS = right side
sl = slip
sl st(s) = slip stitch(es)
ssk = slip, slip, knit (slip each st knitwise, knit both sts tog through the back loops)
st(s) = stitch(es)
St st = stockinette stitch (k 1 row, p 1 row)
tog = together
WS = wrong side

Cuff and Leg

With D, CO 61 sts.
Row 1: K 1, * p 1, k 1; rep from * across.
Row 2: P 1, * k 1, p 1; rep from * across.
Rep rows 1 and 2 with C until 1¼" from beg, ending with a WS row. Then, work in St st following rows 1 through 56 of chart. Next row, k across with A.

Heel

Row 1 (WS): With C, p 15 sts, sl rem sts onto holder, turn.
Row 2: Sl first st, k to end of row, turn.
Rep rows 1 and 2 five more times—12 rows.
Short Rows (WS): P 2, p 2 tog, p 1, turn; sl 1, k 3, turn; p 3, p 2 tog, p 1, turn; sl 1, k 4, turn; p 4, p 2 tog, p 1, turn; sl 1, k 5, turn; p 5, p 2 tog, p 1, turn; sl 1, k 6, turn; p 6, p 2 tog, p 1, turn; sl 1, k 7, turn; p 7, p 2 tog, p 1, turn—9 sts rem.
Break yarn and sl sts onto holder.

Leave center 31 sts on holder for instep and work on rem 15 sts as follows:
Row 1 (RS): With C, k across.

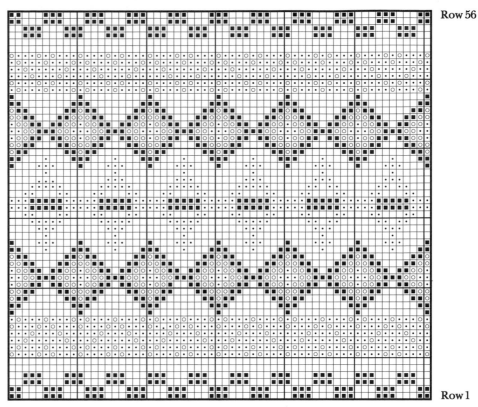

Row 56

Row 1

KNIT STOCKING

Row 2: Sl first st, p to end of row, turn.
Rep rows 1 and 2 five more times—12 rows.
Short Rows (RS): K 2, k 2 tog, k 1, turn; sl 1, p 3, turn; k 3, k 2 tog, k 1, turn; sl 1, p 4, turn; k 4, k 2 tog, k 1, turn; sl 1, p 5, turn; k 5, k 2 tog, k 1, turn; sl 1, p 6, turn; k 6, k 2 tog, k 1, turn; sl 1, p 7, turn; k 7, k 2 tog, k 1, turn—9 sts rem. Break yarn.

Instep and Gussets

Beg with row 6 of chart (WS), p 9 sts from heel, pick up and p 6 sts on side of heel, p 31 sts from holder, pick up and p 6 sts on side of heel, p 9 sts from holder.
Cont following chart rows 7 through 18, then rows 17 down to row 2, while at the same time, shaping as follows and keeping color pattern as consistent as possible:
Row 1 (RS): K 14, k 2 tog, k 29, ssk, k 14—59 sts.
Row 2 and all WS rows: Purl.
Row 3: K 13, k 2 tog, k 29, ssk, k 13—57 sts.
Row 5: K 12, k 2 tog, k 29, ssk, k 12—55 sts.
Row 7: K 11, k 2 tog, k 29, ssk, k 11—53 sts.
Row 9: K 10, k 2 tog, k 29, ssk, k 10—51 sts.
Row 11: K 9, k 2 tog, k 29, ssk, k 9—49 sts.
Cont following chart on rem 49 sts to row 2 of chart, dec 1 st in last row—48 sts.

Toe

Row 1 (RS): With C, k 9, k 2 tog, k 2, ssk, k 18, k 2 tog, k 2, ssk, k 9—44 sts.
Row 2 and all WS rows: P across.

Color Key			
❑	ecru	#430	(A)
■	blue	#315	(B)
•	red	#218	(C)
○	green	#514	(D)

Row 3: K 8, k 2 tog, k 2, ssk, k 16, k 2 tog, k 2, ssk, k 8—40 sts.
Cont as est, dec 4 sts every RS row until 16 sts rem.

Finishing

With right side facing, fold toe so that back seam meets in the center under the foot, and weave together toe sts. Sew back seam.

Loop

With crochet hook and C, ch 16. Sl st in 2nd ch from hook and each ch across. Fasten off and break yarn. Fold chain in half and attach at top back of stocking.

Christmas Afternoon Stocking

DMC	Color
• ⌈ white	white
• ⌊ 032BF Kreinik	pearl
C 928	gray green, lt.
H 927	gray green, med.
∧ 926	gray green, dk.
⋊ 3768	gray green, vy. dk.
◐ 924	gray green, ul. vy. dk.
6 221	pink, vy. dk.
♥ 3721	pink, dk.
X 224	pink, lt.
＼ 225	pink, vy. lt.
Z 3740	antique violet, dk.
⌐ 3041	antique violet, med.
= 3042	antique violet, lt.
∕ 3743	antique violet, vy. lt.
▲ 520	fern green, dk.
♡ 3046	yellow-beige, med.
◑ 930	antique blue, dk.
✦ 931	antique blue, med.
— 3753	antique blue, ul. vy. lt.
⌐ 3752	antique blue, vy. lt.
➘ 500	blue green, vy. dk.
∽ 502	blue green
ε 420	hazelnut, dk.
V 422	hazelnut, lt.
★ 869	hazelnut, vy. dk.
△ 3024	brown gray, vy. lt.
9 647	beaver gray, med.
✳ 645	beaver gray, vy. dk.
∕∕ 844	beaver gray, ul. dk.
◤ 3021	beaver gray, dk.
⌐ 3790	beige gray, ul. dk.
■ 310	black
∣ 3774	flesh, vy. lt.
○ white	white

Fabric: 25-count white Lugana® from Zweigart®
Stitch count: 244H x 140W

Design size:

25-count	19½" x 11¼"
28-count	17½" x 10"
30-count	16¼" x 9⅜"
32-count	15¼" x 8¾"

Instructions: Cross stitch over two threads using two strands of floss. Backstitch using one strand of floss. When floss and Kreinik Metallics are bracketed together, use one strand floss and two strands Kreinik Blending Filament.

Note: Alphabet is included for personalization. Center initials and cross stitch over two threads, using two strands of floss.

Backstitch instructions:
Backstitch in order listed.

3021	tree branches, coat of man skating, pants of boy with dog, harness and reins on horse, jacket of man in sleigh
310	hat of man skating, hat of man in sleigh, eye and nose of dog
930	scarf of skating man, muff of left woman skater, shirt of boy with dog, hat of woman in sleigh, monogram
224	all faces and hands
844	pants of skating man, body and ear of gray horse
645	skates, sled, and ropes
221	hat and skirt of left woman skater
3721	blouse of left woman skater, dress of woman in sleigh
3740	hat of right woman skater, muff of right woman skater, and skirt of right woman skater, jacket of sleigh driver
3046	blouse of right woman skater
520	cap of boy with dog
869	body of tan horse
500	cap of sleigh driver

Materials:
1 yd. 44/45"-wide mauve moiré taffeta (for back, ruffle, and bow)
½ yd. 44/45"-wide white taffeta (for lining)
½ yd. fleece
2 yds. St. Louis Trimming ⅝"-wide metallic antique gold trim
1 yd. St. Louis Trimming 1¾"-wide metallic antique gold trim
2 yds. narrow piping cord
Two 1¼" gold jingle bells
Sewing machine
Threads to match fabric
Hand-sewing needle
Scissors
Measuring tape

1. Complete all cross stitch following instructions given.
2. Pin fleece to wrong side of stitched front. Baste together along perimeter of design, smoothing curves. Cut out stocking ½" beyond basting line.
3. Place stocking front on mauve taffeta with right sides facing and trace around stocking outline. Cut out mauve stocking piece for backing. From mauve taffeta, cut one 5" x 36" strip across fabric width for ruffle, one 6½" x 42" strip across fabric width for bow, one 2¼" x 7" strip for hanging loop, and one 1" x 72" strip, piecing as necessary, to cover piping cord. For lining, use stocking front as a pattern and cut two pieces, reversing one, from white taffeta.
4. Cover piping cord with taffeta strip. Aligning raw edges, sew covered piping to side and bottom edges of stocking front. Repeat to sew ⅝"-wide gold trim on top of piping. With right sides facing and using a ½" seam allowance, sew stocking front and back together, leaving top edge open. Trim seam allowance to ¼", clip curves, and turn.
5. To finish top edge of stocking, gather 1¾"-wide gold trim to fit edge. Aligning raw edges, sew piping and then gold trim around edge. Sew short ends of ruffle strip together and then fold ruffle in half lengthwise with wrong sides facing. Gather bottom ruffle edges to fit top edge of stocking. Sew ruffle around stocking top, aligning raw edges and ruffle seam with back stocking seam. Fold loop strip in half lengthwise with right sides facing and sew long edges together. Trim seam and turn. Sew loop ends to top edge at back seam, aligning raw edges.
6. With right sides facing, sew stocking lining pieces together, leaving top edge open and an opening in the bottom for turning; do not turn. Clip curves. Place stocking inside lining with right sides facing and seams aligned. Sew together along top edges. Pull stocking through opening in bottom of lining. Slipstitch opening closed and insert lining in stocking.
7. Fold taffeta bow strip in half lengthwise, with right sides facing, and cut each short end at an angle. Sew edges together, leaving an opening in one long edge for turning. Trim seam, turn, and slipstitch opening closed. Make a bow with strip and sew to top back edge of stocking front. Sew jingle bells to center of bow.

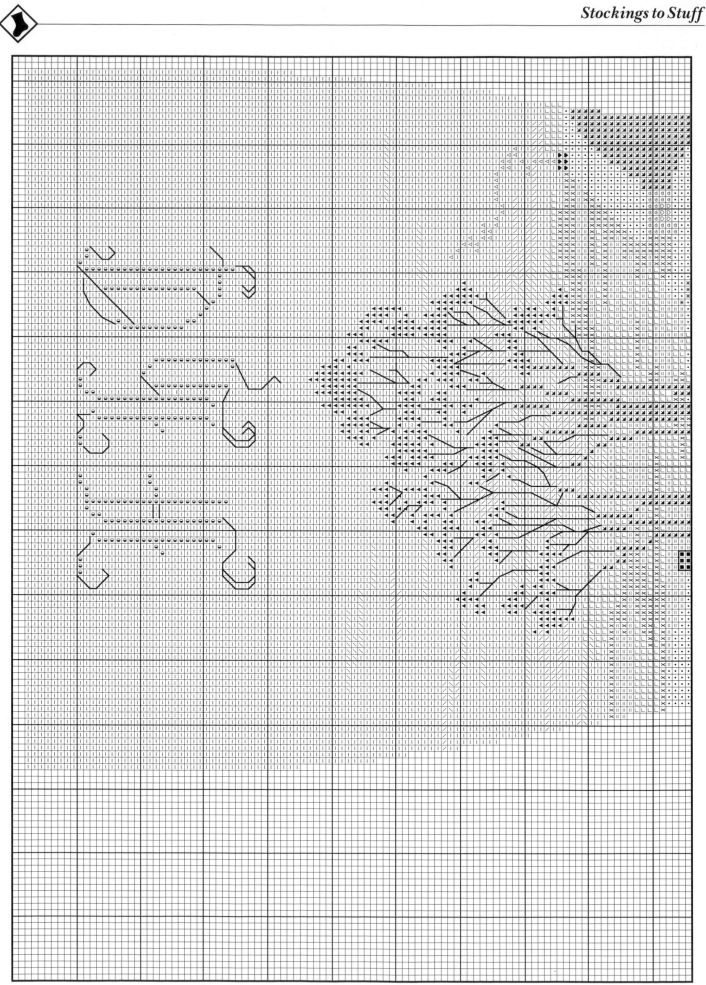

CHRISTMAS AFTERNOON STOCKING (SECTION 1)

Shaded portion indicates overlap from previous page.

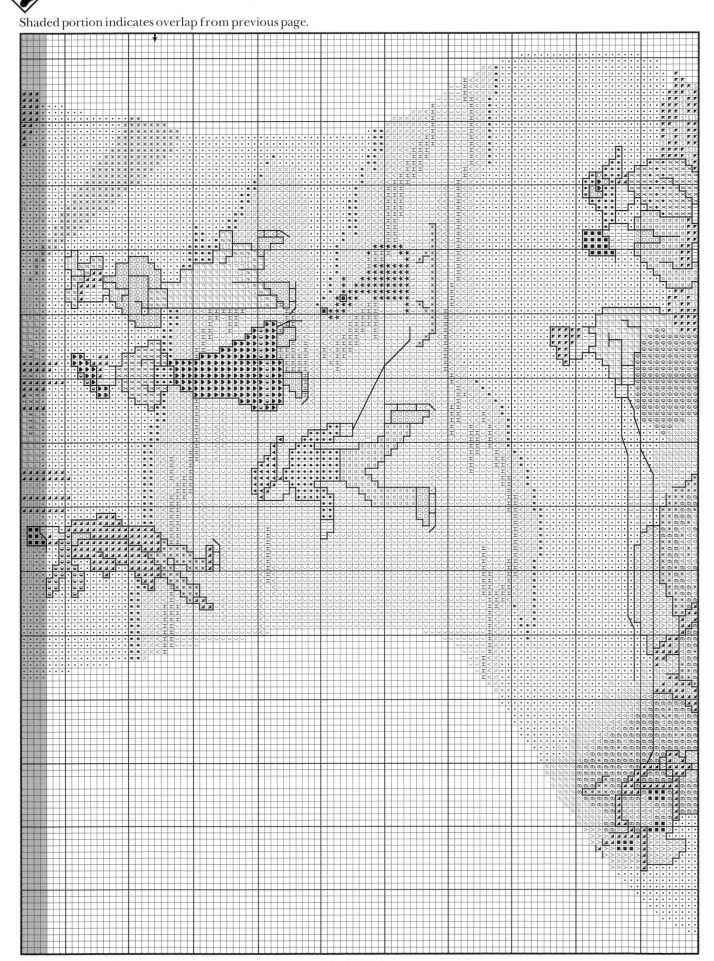

SECTION 2

Shaded portion indicates overlap from previous page.

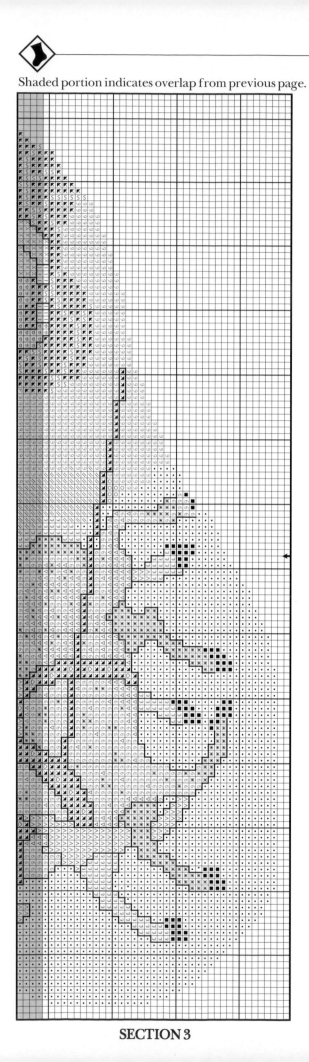

SECTION 3

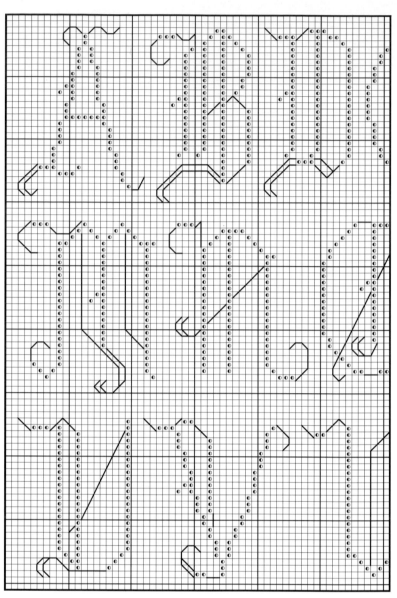

ALPHABET

Shaded portion indicates overlap from previous page.

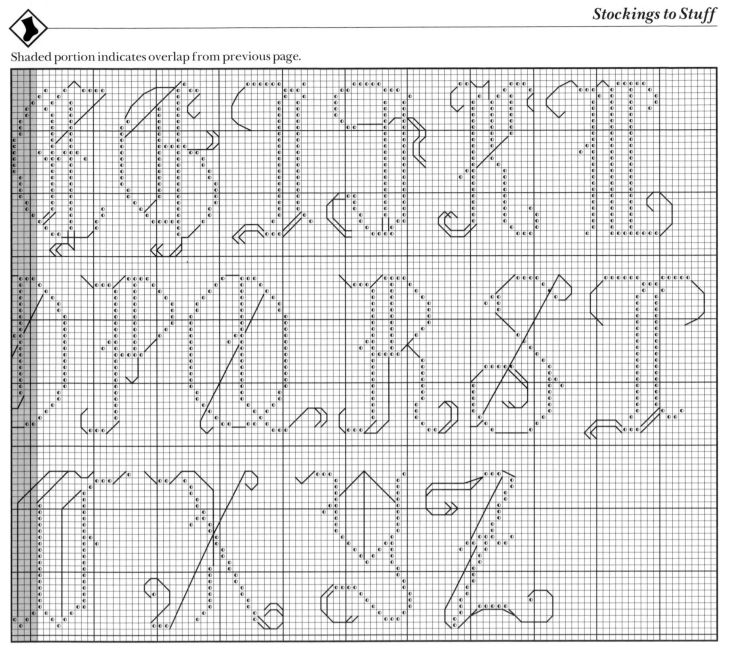

ALPHABET

Yo-Yo Stocking

Note: Unless otherwise indicated, all seam allowances are ¼" and all seams are sewn with right sides facing.

1. Enlarge stocking pattern as indicated. Trace onto tracing paper, adding ¼" seam allowance, and cut out. Cut pieces from fabric as indicated on pattern. From red-and-green print fabric, cut two 5½"x 16" pieces for cuff and cuff lining and one 2 x 5½" strip for hanging loop. Cut one 5½" x 16" cuff piece from fleece.

2. To make fabric circles into yo-yos, stitch around each circle from wrong side of fabric, turning raw edge under ¼" (toward wrong side of fabric) as you work and leaving thread tails long. Pull thread tails tight to form yo-yo, knot thread ends together, and clip close to knot. (See Illustration.)

3. Baste fleece to wrong side of stocking front. Aligning raw edges, sew piping to side and bottom edges of stocking. To attach yo-yos to right side of stocking front, position each yo-yo with gathered side up and a button centered on top. Sew button in place, stitching through yo-yo and stocking. Begin at toe and sew yo-yos close together, overlapping edges, to 4½" from stocking top. Sew stocking front and back together, leaving top edge open. Trim seam, clip curves, and turn.

4. Baste fleece to wrong side of one cuff piece. Fold fleece/cuff piece in half; sew short edges together. Repeat for cuff lining piece. With raw edge of piping toward outside, sew piping around fleece/cuff piece bottom edge on seam line. Align seams and sew bottom edges of cuff and lining together. Trim seam, turn, and press. Baste top edges of cuff together and sew to top of stocking, aligning top edges and seams. Fold loop strip in half lengthwise and sew long edges together. Trim seam and turn. Sew to back seam of cuff, with raw edges of loop at cuff top.

5. Sew stocking lining pieces together, leaving top edge open and an opening in the bottom for turning; do not turn. Clip curves. Place stocking inside lining with right sides facing and seams aligned. Sew together along top edges. Pull stocking through opening in bottom of lining. Slipstitch opening closed and insert lining in stocking.

6. Make a multi-loop bow with red ribbon and sew to center front of cuff. Sew jingle bells and button to cuff below bow center.

**Gathering
Thread**

**Pulled up
and tied.**

ILL.

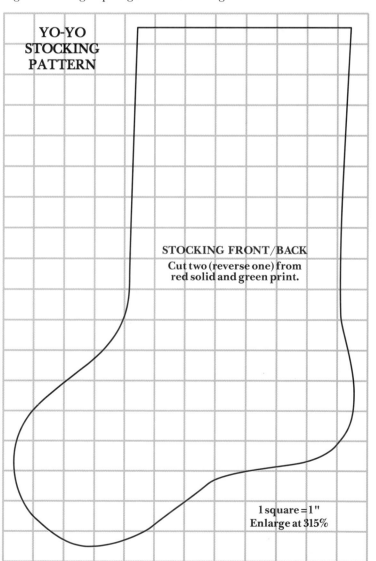

**YO-YO
STOCKING
PATTERN**

STOCKING FRONT/BACK
**Cut two (reverse one) from
red solid and green print.**

**1 square = 1"
Enlarge at 315%**

Gingerbread Stocking

Materials:
Purchased knit Christmas stocking
  with cuff
Duncan Scribbles® 3-Dimensional
  Fabric Writers paint, colors: white,
  bright red, bright green, bright
  yellow, black, bright orange,
  gingersnap, iridescent gold mist
Duncan Scribbles® Soft Fashion Paint,
  color: iridescent golden brown
Size 6 flat fabric paintbrush
Four ⅝" gold jingle bells
Red yarn scraps
Yarn needle
Duncan Scribbles® iron-on transfer
  pencil
Tracing paper

1. Following manufacturer's instructions for transfer pencil, trace pattern and transfer to stocking.
2. Use paintbrush to paint gingerbread boy with iridescent gold mist and let dry. Paint candy cane and peppermint with white and small round candies with bright orange, red, green, and yellow. Let dry.
3. Squeeze paint directly from bottles to paint details and remaining candies. Paint gingerbread boy's eyes and mouth with black and outline with iridescent golden brown. Let dry. Add stitching lines with gingersnap and highlights to mouth and eyes with white. Add red lines to candy cane and peppermint. With black, add shadow lines to gingerbread man and candies.
4. Sew jingle bells to stocking at bottom of cuff using red yarn.

GINGERBREAD STOCKING PATTERNS

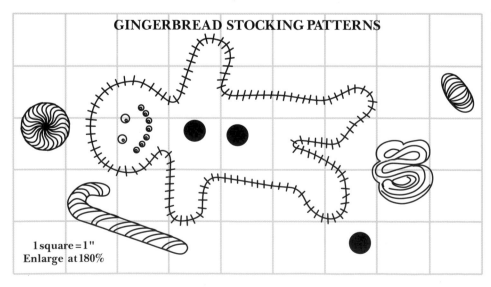

1 square = 1"
Enlarge at 180%

Ornament Stocking

Materials:
15" canvas stocking
Duncan Scribbles® 3-Dimensional
  Fabric Writers paint, colors: white,
  bright green, glittering gold, glittering
  silver, glittering ruby, electric green
Duncan Scribbles® Soft Fashion Paint,
  colors: bright red, bright green
Size 6 flat fabric paintbrush
Duncan Scribbles® iron-on transfer pencil
Tracing paper

1. Following manufacturer's instructions for transfer pencil, trace pattern and transfer to stocking.

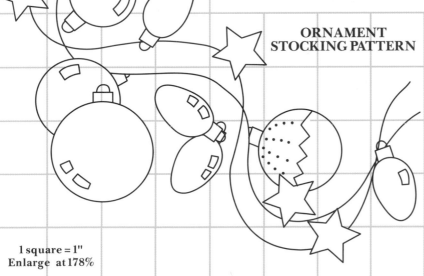

**ORNAMENT
STOCKING PATTERN**

1 square = 1"
Enlarge at 178%

2. Refer to the photo for color placement. Use paintbrush to paint ribbon background with glittering ruby. Paint bulbs and ornaments with bright red and bright green soft fashion paint and glittering silver and electric green dimensional paint. Let dry.

3. Squeeze dimensional paint directly from bottle to complete remaining design areas and details. Add lines to ribbon with glittering ruby. Paint lined stars, bulbs, and ornaments with glitter paints, spacing lines close together, but not touching, to fill in shapes. Add decorative dots or lines to ornaments as desired. Paint ornament caps with glittering gold and silver and hooks with glittering silver. Paint highlights with white.

Keepsakes for Someone Special

One of the very best parts of the Christmas season is the spirit of giving, and crafters and stitchers seem to embody that spirit, long before the calendar reads December. Creating gifts by hand that will be treasured for a lifetime, whether with needle and floss or with crafting materials and glue, brings pleasure to both the givers and the receivers.

On the following pages is a variety of small samplings that will be splendid for stuffing the stockings of everyone on your gift list. From the darling Annie Apple Doll (great for little girls and big girls too) to a crazy-quilt memory book for Mom to knitted golf club covers for Dad, this assortment will please young and old alike.

Embroidered Hearts

Materials:
12" x 18" piece rose velvet fabric
2 yds. Capitol Imports 1"-wide ivory
    Cluny lace (cut into 24" lengths)
⅔ yd. ¼"-wide gold metallic ribbon
    (cut into 8" lengths)
Polyester fiberfill
Dressmaker's carbon paper
Tracing paper
Pencil
Sewing machine
Scissors

Note: Materials will make three hearts.

1. Trace patterns. Transfer fronts and three backs lightly to right side of velvet fabric using dressmaker's carbon. Follow instructions below and stitch illustrations on page **141** to embroider designs. Cut out hearts along outlines.
2. For **each** heart, overlap and sew ends of one lace length together. Run a gathering stitch along straight edge of lace, ¼" from edge. Pin overlapped lace ends to center top of heart front, aligning raw edges and gathering to fit. Sew lace around perimeter of heart. Using a ¼" seam allowance and with right sides facing, sew heart front and back pieces together, leaving opening for turning. Clip curved edges and turn. Stuff firmly and slipstitch opening closed. Make loop with gold ribbon and sew to top back of heart.

Anchor®	DMC	Color
275	746	off white
38	335	rose, dk.
36	3326	rose, lt.
846	3051	olive green
—	282	gold metallic thread

Note: Models were stitched using Anchor® embroidery floss.

Instructions: Make stitches using two strands of floss or metallic thread unless otherwise indicated. Follow natural direction of petals and leaves when stitching. Make French knots using two strands gold metallic thread, wrapping thread around needle twice.

Split stitch instructions:

746	275	outlines and insides of letters
3051	846	stems, outlines of leaves
335	38	outlines of flowers (one strand)

Straight stitch instructions:

3326	36	flower petals
3051	846	leaves

Fly stitch instructions:

3051	846	base of buds

French knot instructions:

282	—	flower centers, dots around design

EMBROIDERED HEARTS PATTERNS

1 square = 1"
Enlarge at 188%

Leave open.

FRONT 1

Leave open.

FRONT 2

Leave open.

FRONT 3

BACK

STITCH KEY

—— = Cutting line	Leaves =	Outline and filling
- - - = Stitching line	Flowers =	Long center stitch
····· = French knots		2 straight stitches on each
Lettering = Split stitch	✿	side to form petal shape.
Stems = Split stitch		Outline with split stitch single strand.

Quilted Star Book Cover
& Star Mini-Quilt

Quilted Star Book Cover

Materials:
Purchased paperback book
½ yd. 44/45"-wide floral print fabric
  (for cover)
2¾" square ivory print fabric
  (for block background)
1" x 2" strip **each** of four coordinating
  print fabrics (for star)
Coordinating single-fold bias tape
7" x 10" piece fleece
Four 1" x 2" strips Therm O Web
  HeatnBond™ Lite iron-on adhesive
Therm O Web HeatnBond™ Lite ⅜"-
  wide iron-on adhesive tape
Rotary cutter and mat
Quilter's clear plastic ruler
Threads to match fabrics
Scissors   Straight pins
Measuring tape   Sewing machine

1. From floral background fabric, cut
two 7¼" x 3" pieces along selvage edge
for book cover pockets and two 7¼" x
10¼" pieces for the cover and lining.
2. Following manufacturer's instructions, fuse iron-on adhesive strips to
wrong side of 1" x 2" fabric strips; do not
remove paper backing. Using rotary
cutter and mat, place each strip on mat
with paper side up and precision-cut to
½" x 2". Using the quilter's ruler and rotary cutter, cut two diamonds from each
color strip as shown in Illustration 1. Remove paper backing. Fuse eight diamonds to center of ivory print square
with like colors opposite to form a star.
3. Cut four 3¼" lengths **each** from bias
tape and iron-on adhesive. Fuse adhesive to wrong side of bias tape. Remove
paper backing. See Illustration 2 and
position ivory print square on floral
cover piece. Center and fuse bias tape
strips over edges of square.

4. Layer cover lining piece (right-side-
down), fleece, and appliquéd cover
(right-side-up) and pin. Machine appliqué edges of diamonds and bias strips
using a narrow zigzag stitch. For each diamond, use matching thread and begin
stitching at center of star. Stitch three
edges of diamond, but do not stitch
fourth edge; fourth edge will be covered
when edges of next diamond are stitched.
Repeat to finish all diamond edges.
5. Remove pins and place cover over
paperback book to shape. Pin layers together while in folded position over
book. Remove cover from book and
baste edges together ⅛" from edge.
6. Pin and baste one pocket piece right-
side-up to each end of cover lining. Position each pocket with raw edges
aligned with lining edges and selvage
edge toward center of cover.
7. Cut a 6" length of bias tape for a
bookmark. Fold in half lengthwise with
wrong sides facing and turn under one
short end to hem. Topstitch edges together. Baste unhemmed short edge of
tape to center top edge of cover lining.
8. Beginning and ending at center bottom of cover, sew bias tape over edges,
mitering corners.

Star Mini-Quilt

Quilt size: 11½" x 11½"

Materials:
Two 12" squares sea-foam green print
  fabric (for border and backing)
9" square floral print fabric (for
  background)
Four 2¾" squares ivory print fabric (for
  block background)
Four 1" x 4" strips **each** of four
  coordinating print fabrics (for star)
Coordinating single-fold bias tape
12" square fleece
Four 1" x 4" strips Therm O Web
  HeatnBond™ Lite iron-on adhesive
Therm O Web HeatnBond™ Lite ⅜"-
  wide iron-on adhesive tape
Rotary cutter and mat
Quilter's clear plastic ruler
Sewing machine
Threads to match fabrics
Scissors
Measuring tape
Straight pins

1. Follow steps 2 and 3 of *Star Book
Cover* to cut diamond pieces and fuse a
star to center of each ivory square.
2. Position ivory squares on point on
floral background fabric with points
½" from edge and ¼" from each other.
Pin in place. Layer one sea-foam green
square (right-side-down), fleece remaining sea-foam green square (right-side-
up), and floral background square
(centered and right-side-up). Pin layers
together. Machine-quilt horizontally
and vertically across center of floral
background square.
3. Cut four 9", four 3½", and four 9⅜"
lengths **each** of bias tape and adhesive tape. Fuse tape to wrong side of
bias strips and remove paper backing.
Position 9" strips across background
block diagonally, covering raw edges
of the ivory blocks; fuse in place. Fuse
3½" strips over remaining ivory block
edges. Position and fuse 9⅜" strips
over edges of floral background
fabric.
4. Follow step 4 of *Star Book Cover* to
appliqué star edges. Topstitch along
edges of bias tape strips, stitching close
to the edge.
5. Bind raw edges with bias tape,
stitching close to edge.

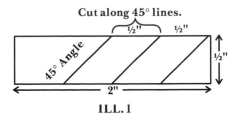

ILL. 1

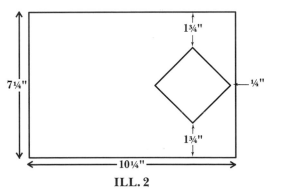

ILL. 2

Furry Friends

Catnip Mouse

Materials:
12" square homespun cotton fabric
Scrap of brown felt
1 yd. 3-ply worsted-weight light brown
    yarn (cut into 12" lengths)
Dried catnip leaf
Yarn needle
Threads to match fabrics
Sewing machine (optional)
Tracing paper
Pencil

Note: Unless otherwise indicated, all seam allowances are ¼" and all seams are sewn with right sides facing.

1. Trace patterns onto tracing paper, transferring markings. Cut from fabric as indicated on patterns.
2. Run a gathering thread across each ear, pull thread tightly to gather, and knot to secure.

3. Pin mouse body pieces together with ears between as indicated on pattern. Sew together, leaving bottom open. Sew bottom piece to sides, leaving open as indicated. Turn.

4. Stuff mouse firmly with dried catnip. Fold under raw edges and slipstitch opening closed.

5. To add tail, align three yarn lengths and thread yarn needle. Insert needle at right of back seam and pull out at left of back seam, ¾" above bottom seam. Pull yarn until even on both sides. Braid yarn tightly and tie an overhand knot to end.

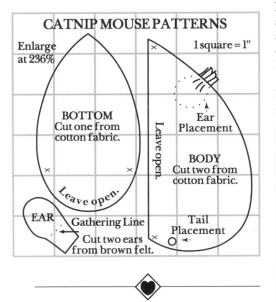

CATNIP MOUSE PATTERNS

Enlarge at 236%

1 square = 1"

BOTTOM
Cut one from cotton fabric.

BODY
Cut two from cotton fabric.

Leave open.

Ear Placement

Tail Placement

Gathering Line

Leave open.

EAR
Cut two ears from brown felt.

Cat Quilt

Quilt size: 28" x 28"

Materials:
1¼ yds. 44/45"-wide light yellow print fabric (for background and backing)
¼ yd. 44/45"-wide tan print fabric (for cat's face)
¼ yd. **each** three different 44/45"-wide gray print fabrics (for mice)
½ yd. 44/45"-wide dark pink print fabric (for border)
⅝ yd. 44/45"-wide blue print fabric (for binding)
2" x 4" piece green print fabric (for pupils of eyes)
3" x 6" piece dark yellow print fabric (for eyes)
4" x 8" piece peach print fabric (for inner ears and nose)
3" x 6" piece gray Ultrasuede® fabric or felt (for mice ears)
2¼ yds. green piping
30"-square piece batting
Embroidery floss, colors: brown, black, gray, pink

Two ⅝" white buttons (for cat's eyes)
Quilter's template plastic
Dressmaker's marking pen
Rotary cutter and cutting mat
Quilter's clear plastic ruler
Threads to match fabrics
Hand-sewing needle
Tapestry needle
Scissors
Tracing paper
Pencil
Sewing machine
Straight pins
Iron

Note: Unless otherwise indicated, all seam allowances are ¼" and all seams are sewn with right sides facing. Use log cabin method to assemble quilt top. Press all seams toward darker fabrics.

1. Using the rotary cutter, mat, and quilter's ruler, cut 2½" squares as follows:

37 squares from light yellow print fabric, 52 squares from dark pink print fabric, 27 squares from tan print fabric, and four squares from **each** of the three gray print fabrics. These squares include ¼" seam allowance. From blue print fabric, cut four 1½" x 30" strips for binding.

2. Trace mouse ear pattern onto tracing paper, cut out. Cut ear pieces from Ultrasuede® as indicated on pattern. Trace template patterns onto template plastic and cut out. Add ¼" seam allowances to templates when cutting from fabric. Using large triangle template, cut eight triangles from light yellow print fabric, 16 triangles from tan print fabric, four triangles from peach print fabric, 24 triangles from dark pink print fabric, and eight triangles from **each** of the three gray print fabrics. Using half-triangle template, cut four triangles **each** from dark yellow print and green print fabrics, and one triangle

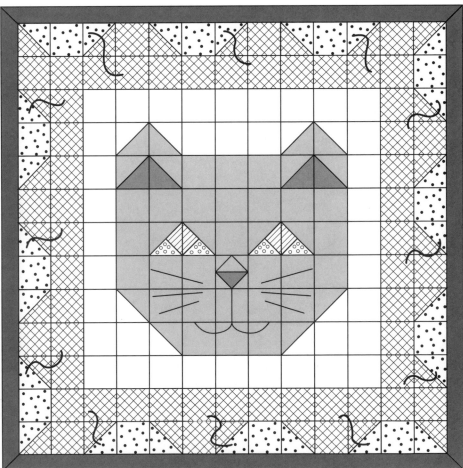

CAT QUILT ASSEMBLY DIAGRAM

COLOR KEY	
Tan print fabric	Dark pink print fabric
Light yellow print fabric	Blue print fabric
Peach print fabric	Dark yellow print fabric
Gray print fabric	Green print fabric

each from peach print and tan print fabrics. Using quarter-triangle template, cut four triangles from tan print fabric.

3. Refer to photo, Quilt Assembly Diagram, and color key to piece quilt top. Piece squares and triangles for cat head and yellow background to make center panel. Sew green piping around perimeter of center panel. Piece mouse border panels, making a pleat in straight edge of each ear and catching ear in seam of gray head and dark pink triangles. Sew borders to center panel. Layer backing (right-side-down), batting, and quilt top (centered and right-side-up). Pin and baste through all layers. Machine-quilt in-the-ditch around cat head and inner edge of border.

4. Using the dressmaker's marking pen, lightly draw a tail on each mouse and whiskers and mouth on the cat. For each mouse, machine satin-stitch tail with gray thread. For each mouse, use the tapestry needle to make a large French knot with black embroidery floss for eye, and hand satin-stitch nose with pink embroidery floss. For whiskers, sew one 3" length of gray floss above nose and knot center; trim ends to 1". For cat, embroider whiskers and mouth using a stem stitch and brown embroidery floss. Sew on buttons for cat's eyes.

5. Trim batting and backing even with quilt top.

CAT QUILT TEMPLATES

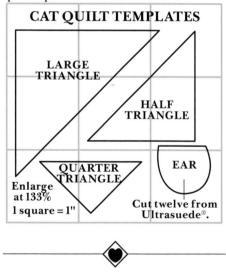

LARGE TRIANGLE

HALF TRIANGLE

QUARTER TRIANGLE

EAR

Enlarge at 133%
1 square = 1"

Cut twelve from Ultrasuede®.

Dog Quilt

Quilt size: 33½" x 33½"

Materials:
1¾ yds. 44/45"-wide blue print fabric (for bone blocks and backing)
¾ yd. 44/45"-wide yellow solid fabric (for hydrant blocks)

⅓yd. each three different 44/45"-wide red print fabrics (for hydrants)
¼ yd. 44/45"-wide red print fabric (for binding)
¼ yd. 44/45"-wide white solid fabric (for bones)
1 yd. Pellon® Wonder-Under® Transfer Fusing Web
Threads to match and contrast with fabrics
Black embroidery floss
36"-square piece batting
Pencil
Hand-sewing needle
Tapestry needle
Scissors
Sewing machine
Straight pins
Iron
Tracing paper

Note: Unless otherwise indicated, all seam allowances are ¼" and all seams are sewn with right sides facing.

1. From blue print fabric, cut four 11½" squares for bone blocks and one 36" square for backing. From yellow solid fabric, cut five 11½" squares. From red print fabric, cut four 1½" x 36" strips.

2. Following manufacturer's instructions, trace patterns for five hydrants, four large bones, four medium bones, and three small bones onto transfer web paper. Fuse patterns to wrong side of appropriate fabrics and cut out. Referring to photo, center and fuse a fire hydrant to each yellow block and two or three bones to each blue print block. Machine satin-stitch hydrant edges and detail lines with red thread and bone edges with black thread. Hand-embroider names of choice on bones using black embroidery floss and a stem stitch.

3. Refer to photo and sew blocks together in three rows of three blocks each. Sew rows together and press seams toward blue print blocks. Layer backing (right-side-down), batting, and quilt top (centered and right-side-up). Pin and baste through all layers. Machine-quilt in-the-ditch along seam lines. Tie corners of center block with black floss.

4. Trim batting and backing even with quilt top. Sew binding strips to sides of quilt top, aligning raw edges and mitering corners. Turn binding to back of quilt, press under raw edges, and slipstitch in place.

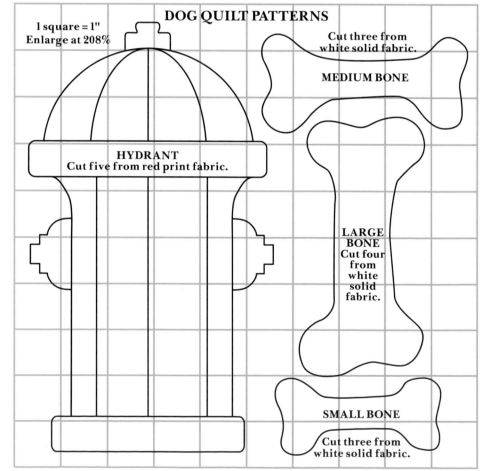

1 square = 1"
Enlarge at 208%

DOG QUILT PATTERNS

HYDRANT
Cut five from red print fabric.

Cut three from white solid fabric.
MEDIUM BONE

LARGE BONE
Cut four from white solid fabric.

SMALL BONE
Cut three from white solid fabric.

Clown Scissors Keeper

Materials:

2½" x 6" piece black-and-white striped fabric

8" square black with white dot fabric

3" square white with black dot fabric

6" square white solid fabric

1 yd. 1½"-wide black-and-white striped satin ribbon

¾ yd. ⅜"-wide red curly grosgrain ribbon

1 yd. red jumbo rickrack

Two 12- x 10-mm. yellow heart pony beads

6-mm wood coco beads: 1 red, 15 yellow

Two 4-mm black round beads

Polyester fiberfill

Threads to match fabrics

Fine-tip permanent black marker

Tracing paper   Pencil   Scissors

Note: Unless otherwise indicated, all seam allowances are ⅜" and all seams are sewn with right sides facing.

1. Trace patterns onto tracing paper and cut out. Cut pieces from fabric as indicated on patterns. From striped fabric, cut two 3½" x 2½" strips for arms.

2. Sew hat to top of head and head to top of body; fold piece in half and sew long edges together. Turn under raw edges at bottom of body and sew a gathering stitch along edge. Stuff firmly, pull gathering thread tightly, and knot ends to secure. Sew feet pieces together around edges. Clip a small **X** in center of one piece, and turn. Stuff feet lightly and topstitch down center from point to point as indicated on pattern. Sew feet to bottom of body. To make each arm, fold one 3½" x 2½" strip in half with short edges together, sew seam, and turn. Turn ends under ¼" and sew gathering thread along each edge. Pull tightly to gather and knot thread ends. Sew arms to clown at sides.

3. Sew red curly ribbon to top and bottom of hat, around collar, down front of body, and around ends of arms for cuffs. Sew a heart button to end of each arm for a hand. Referring to photo, sew red bead to center of face for nose and black beads to face for eyes. Use marker to draw smiling mouth. Sew yellow beads around sides and back of head for hair.

4. Sew rickrack along center front of black-and-white striped ribbon. With rickrack side up, turn under one short end of ribbon and sew to back of clown at waistline. Turn under end and edges of remaining end to fit through scissors handle and slipstitch in place.

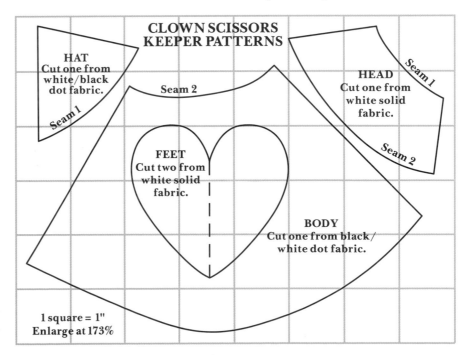

CLOWN SCISSORS KEEPER PATTERNS

HAT Cut one from white/black dot fabric.

Seam 1

Seam 2

HEAD Cut one from white solid fabric.

Seam 1

Seam 2

FEET Cut two from white solid fabric.

BODY Cut one from black/white dot fabric.

1 square = 1"
Enlarge at 173%

Annie Apple Doll

Materials:
1 yd. 44/45"-wide red with white dots fabric
½ yd. 44/45"-wide white solid fabric
½ yd. 44/45"-wide muslin fabric
6" square red solid fabric
¾ yd. ½"-wide white gathered eyelet lace
Acrylic paint, colors: brown, green
Liner paintbrush
Four ⅝" white buttons
Fine-tip permanent black marker
Threads to match fabrics
Hand-sewing needle
Polyester fiberfill   Pencil
Hot glue gun   Iron
Sewing machine   Scissors
Measuring tape   Tracing paper

Note: Unless otherwise indicated, all seam allowances are ¼" and all seams are sewn with right sides facing.

1. Trace patterns onto tracing paper, transferring markings, and cut out. Cut pieces from fabric as indicated on patterns. From red/white dot fabric, cut one 8½" x 24" piece for skirt, two 3½" x 4" pieces for bodice, and two 9½" x 6" pieces for sleeves. From white fabric, cut one 11½" x 6" piece for apron skirt, two 2½" x 3" pieces for apron bib, and one 5½" x 1½" piece for apron waistband.

2. Use the marker to draw eyes and mouth on face. Hand-appliqué two small apples to cheeks.

3. Sew body front and back together, leaving opening in bottom for turning. Turn and stuff firmly with fiberfill. Slipstitch opening closed. Sew each pair of arm and leg pieces together, leaving ends open for turning. Turn pieces and stuff firmly with fiberfill. Slipstitch openings closed. Sew arms and legs to body as indicated on patterns.

4. To make apron skirt, turn under ¼" twice on one long edge and both short edges, and topstitch in place. Evenly space and hand-appliqué three small apples across skirt, 1½" above hemmed long edge. Fold apron waistband in half with wrong sides facing. Gather top edge of apron skirt to fit waistband and sew in place, aligning raw edges. Sew apron bib pieces together, leaving bottom short edge open. Turn and press. Sew bottom edge of bib to center back of waistband. Hand appliqué large apple to center front of apron bib.

5. Refer to Illustration and sew top 4" edges of bodice together for ½" on each side. Gather one 6" edge on each sleeve and sew to bodice. Sew bodice side seams and sleeve seams. Sew short edges of skirt piece together and gather top long edge. Pull gathers to fit bodice and sew in place. Press under ¼" on bottom edge of skirt; topstitch eyelet to wrong side. Position apron on dress front; sew one button to each top corner of bib and to each end of apron waistband.

6. Place dress on doll. Turn under neck edges and tack to doll. Turn under sleeve ends and gather to fit arms; knot gathering threads to secure.

7. Sew pantaloon pieces together along crotch seam. Sew leg seams. Slip pantaloons on doll. Turn under top and leg edges and gather to fit doll; knot gathering threads.

8. Tear ¼"-wide strips of red fabric and cut 18 (4") lengths. Knot centers of strips together in sets of two. Hot glue knots across top and sides of head, as indicated by large X's on pattern.

9. Use the paintbrush to paint apple stems with brown and leaves with green.

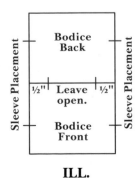

ILL.

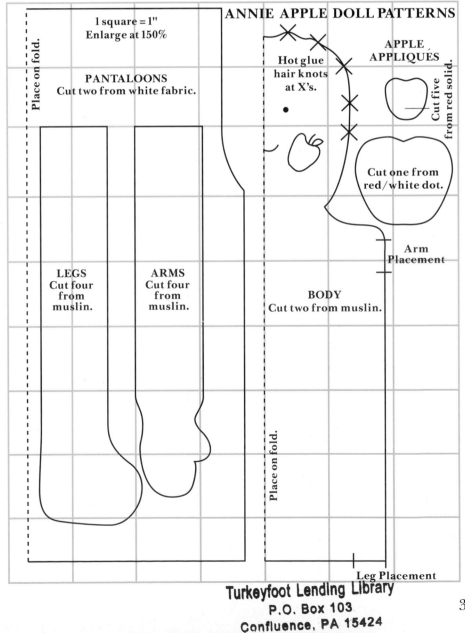

ANNIE APPLE DOLL PATTERNS

1 square = 1"
Enlarge at 150%

PANTALOONS
Cut two from white fabric.

Place on fold.

APPLE APPLIQUÉS

Hot glue hair knots at X's.

Cut five from red solid.

Cut one from red/white dot.

Arm Placement

LEGS
Cut four from muslin.

ARMS
Cut four from muslin.

BODY
Cut two from muslin.

Place on fold.

Leg Placement

Bags for All Occasions

Grandma's Treasure Bag

Trellis Lunch Bag

Trellis Lunch Bag

Stenciled Sachet Bag

Materials:
7" x 12¼"canvas lunch bag
Duncan Scribbles® Soft Fashion Paint,
  colors: Wedgwood blue, evergreen,
  chiffon green, black
Duncan Scribbles® 3-Dimensional
Fabric Writers Paint, colors: white,
  bright yellow, delicate rose, golden
  pearl, paradise sunset
Paintbrush sizes: 4 liner, 5 round,
  ½" shader

Small sea sponge	White chalk
¾"-wide masking tape	Stylus
Tracing paper	Pencil
Aluminum foil	Ruler

1. Use strips of masking tape to make a trellis design on bottom 4¾" of bag front. Place tape strips diagonally from bottom right to upper left, spacing ¾" apart. Repeat to add diagonal strips from bottom left to upper right. Press tape edges down firmly.
2. Paint squares of canvas between tape strips chiffon green using the shader brush. Shade the left side of each

40

square with Wedgwood blue. Let dry. Remove top layer of tape strips. Use Wedgwood blue to shade unpainted squares along edge of remaining tape. Let dry and remove tape.

3. Pour a quarter-size amount of evergreen and small amounts each of black and bright yellow onto foil. Dampen sponge and squeeze out excess water. Dab sponge into evergreen and dip a small corner of sponge in black. Dab sponge on foil to blend slightly, and then sponge color on bag in a triangular-shaped area at top of trellis design. Without cleaning sponge, dip into yellow and dab on foil to blend. Sponge highlights over green area on bag; let dry. Clean sponge.

4. Trace flower pattern and use chalk to draw over pattern lines on back of paper. Position pattern chalk side down on bag and retrace lines with stylus to transfer pattern.

5. To paint leaves, load round brush with evergreen and dip sparingly in black. Brush on foil to blend slightly and paint shaded side of each leaf from base toward the point. Clean brush, and repeat with evergreen and bright yellow to paint light side of each leaf.

6. To paint large flowers, squeeze white and delicate rose onto foil. Load round brush with delicate rose, dip sparingly in white, and brush on foil to blend slightly. Paint comma-stroke petals from outside to center of each flower, reloading brush as necessary. Let dry. Add dots of bright yellow directly from bottle for flower centers.

7. Thin a small amount of black to an inky consistency and use the liner brush to randomly outline leaves. Paint tendrils with thinned evergreen. Load liner with evergreen, dip sparingly in black, and paint shaded areas of tendrils. Repeat with evergreen and bright yellow to paint highlighted areas of tendrils.

8. Applying paint directly from bottle, make a small dot of paradise sunset in each filler flower center, and add dots at ends of several tendrils. Add five or six dots of golden pearl around each filler flower center. Let dry 24 hours.

Stenciled Sachet Bag

Materials:

4" x 6" piece **each** unbleached muslin and mauve striped cotton fabric
¼ yd. 1"-wide ecru Cluny lace trim
½ yd. ⅛"-wide mauve satin ribbon
Acrylic paint, colors: mauve, sage green
1½ cups dried lavender buds or potpourri of choice
Two small pieces of sponge
4" x 5" sheet stencil plastic
Sharp craft knife
Smooth cutting board
Fine-tip permanent black marker
Threads to match fabrics
Scissors
Iron
Masking tape
Sewing machine (optional)
Waxed paper   Paper towels

1. Place stencil plastic over pattern and trace with marker. Tape plastic to cutting board and use craft knife to carefully cut out design.

2. Center stencil on muslin piece, with bottom of design 1" above one short edge of fabric.

3. Pour a small amount of green paint onto a sheet of waxed paper. Dip sponge in paint and blot on paper towel to remove excess. Holding stencil firmly in place, sponge-paint leaf area with green. Using a clean sponge, repeat to apply mauve to flower area of stencil. Let paint dry thoroughly. Press on wrong side with warm iron to heat-set.

4. Place muslin and mauve striped fabric pieces with right sides together. Using a ¼" seam, sew pieces together across bottom and up one side edge. Turn top edge under and press. Sew lace trim around top edge. Place right sides together and sew remaining side seam. Turn and press.

5. Fill bag with lavender buds or potpourri and tie top closed with ribbon.

Grandma's Treasure Bag

Materials:

5"-square canvas tote
Faultless Starch/Bon Ami Solutions™ fabric glue
Color photocopies of two photographs, each trimmed to a 2¼" circle
Tulip dimensional fabric paint, colors: gold pearl, turquoise
Two ½" white ribbon roses
Six novelty buttons
Medium-size fabric paintbrush
Iron
Press cloth

1. Apply a ⅛"-thick coat of fabric glue to front of one photocopy; place face down on center of bag front. Rub from center out to remove air bubbles. Let dry. Use a warm iron and press cloth to heat-set for 10 to 15 seconds. Soak in cool water for 3 minutes, remove, and gently rub off paper. Rinse and let dry. Repeat soaking and rubbing if any paper remains, and let dry. Repeat to apply remaining photocopy to back of bag.

2. Squeezing paint directly from bottle, outline picture with gold pearl. Write message above picture and add small heart and dots to bag and handle with turquoise. Let dry and outline photo on bag back with gold pearl. Let dry.

3. Glue ribbon roses and buttons to bag.

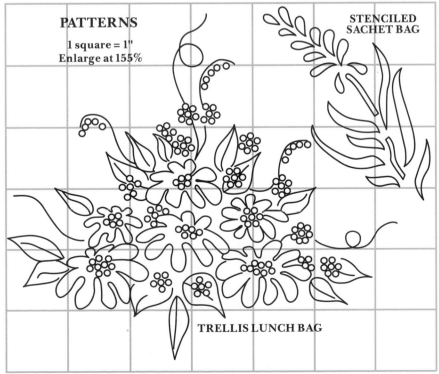

PATTERNS

1 square = 1"
Enlarge at 155%

STENCILED SACHET BAG

TRELLIS LUNCH BAG

Jar Lid Covers & Watch Pincushion

Jar Lid Covers

You Are Special

DMC		Color
●	321	red
\	699	green
X	744	yellow, pl.
+	334	baby blue, med.
V	336	navy
■	3371	black-brown

Fabric: 14-count white Aida from Charles Craft, Inc.

Stitch count: 27H x 26W

Design size:

11-count	2½" x 2⅜"
14-count	1⅞" x 1⅞"
18-count	1½" x 1½"
22-count	1¼" x 1⅛"

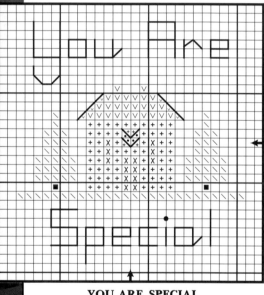

YOU ARE SPECIAL

FOR MY GUY

For My Guy

DMC		Color
•	319	pistachio, vy. dk.
∨	920	copper, med.
X	744	yellow, pl.
+	801	coffee, dk.
−	422	hazelnut, lt.
o	453	shell gray, lt.
△	white	white
bs	336	navy
bs	3371	black-brown

Fabric: 14-count white Aida from Charles Craft, Inc.
Stitch count: 26H x 34W
Design size:

11-count	2⅜" x 3⅛"
14-count	1⅞" x 2⅜"
18-count	1½" x 1⅞"
22-count	1⅛" x 1½"

Instructions: Cross stitch using two strands of floss. Backstitch using one strand of floss unless otherwise indicated.

Backstitch (bs) instructions:

336	water, roof of house
744	heart on house
3371	lettering (two strands), remainder of backstitching

Materials (for **each** jar lid cover):
8" circle pindot cotton fabric
16" length ½"-wide coordinating bias tape
10" length ¼"-wide elastic
2½" circle fusible webbing
Pint jar with lid
Green sewing thread
1½" x 3" piece index card
Stamps: "To," "From," hearts in row
Red and green stamp ink pads
22" length ⅛"-wide coordinating satin
    ribbon
Hole punch
Sewing machine
Scissors   Iron

1. Complete all cross stitch following instructions given.
2. With cross stitch design centered, cut one 2½" circle from Aida fabric. Following manufacturer's instructions for fusible webbing, fuse Aida circle to center of cotton fabric circle. Machine satin-stitch Aida edges with green thread.
3. Sew a ¼" hem around fabric circle. On wrong side of fabric, sew bias tape around circle, 1" from hemmed edge, to form casing. Insert elastic through casing and sew ends together. Adjust gathers and fit cover over jar lid.
4. To make the tag, punch hole in upper left corner of index card. Stamp card with ink and tie onto jar lid with ribbon. Tie ribbon ends into a bow.

Watch Pincushion

Kreinik #8 Braid		Color
■	005HL	black
X	003	red
╱	003	red (**half cross**)
	029	turquoise

Fabric: 14-count white Aida from Zweigart®
Stitch count: 41H x 41W
Design size: 14-count   2⅞" x 2⅞"

Instructions: Cross stitch using one strand braid. Work half cross stitches and backstitch using one strand of braid. Make Algerian eye stitches, using one strand 029 and referring to stitch illustration on page 141. Make French knots in center of Algerian eye stitches, using one strand 005HL and wrapping braid around needle once.
Backstitch instructions:

005HL	watch hands
003	outer edge of watch face

Materials:
5"-square red fabric (for backing)
½ yd. ⅞"-wide black grosgrain ribbon
⅜" black button with shank
1½" piece black Velcro® (for closure)
2½" circle cut from plastic coffee-can lid
Polyester fiberfill
Hand-sewing needle
#24 tapestry needle
Sewing machine   Scissors
Threads to match fabrics   Iron

1. Complete all stitching following instructions.
2. Trim Aida to ½" from stitched design.

Cut backing fabric to same size as stitched front.
3. Place front and backing pieces with right sides together, aligning edges. Sew pieces together, using a ½" seam allowance and leaving a 1½" opening. Trim seam, clip curves, and turn. Insert plastic circle and stuff firmly with fiberfill. Slipstitch opening closed. Sew button to seam at right of the numeral 3.
4. To make the watchband, fold ribbon in half crosswise, aligning raw edges and turning under cut ends; press. Stitching close to the edge, machine-stitch the two layers together along all four edges. Sew Velcro® to ends for closure.
5. Center and slipstitch watchband to back of stitched watch.

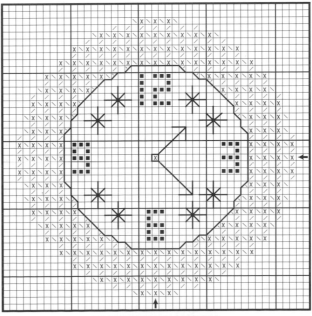

WATCH PINCUSHION

Teacher's Eraser

DMC		Color
•	white	white
╲	948	peach flesh, vy. lt.
C	727	topaz, vy. lt.
H	3766	peacock, lt.
◤	806	peacock, dk.
⌐	352	coral, lt.
╲	350	coral, med.
◐	434	brown, lt.
Fk	3765	peacock, vy. dk.

Fabric: 14-count peach Aida from Charles Craft, Inc.

Stitch count: 26H x 62W
Design size:

11-count	2⅜" x 5⅝"
14-count	1⅞" x 4½"
18-count	1½" x 3½"
22-count	1⅛" x 2⅞"

Instructions: Cross stitch using two strands of floss. Backstitch using one strand of floss unless otherwise indicated. Make French knots using one strand of floss, wrapping floss around needle twice.

Backstitch instructions:

350	girl's dress, bird's beak (two strands)
434	land on globe, bird, girl's shoe
3765	outside edge of globe, letters, back of book (two strands)
3766	pages of book
727	girl's hair

French knot (Fk) instructions:

806	girl's eyes
3765	bird's eye

Materials:
2" x 5" chalkboard eraser
½ yd. ⅜"-wide peach braid trim
½ yd. blue rattail cord
2" x 5" piece regular-loft fleece
Two 2" x 5" pieces extra-loft fleece
Thick craft glue
Peach and blue chalk sticks
Scissors   Thread to match fabric

1. Center regular loft fleece on wrong side of stitched design and baste together along edges of fleece. Topstitch ¼" beyond fleece to stitch a 2½" x 5½" rectangle. Trim cross-stitch fabric ½" beyond stitched line.
2. Glue two layers of extra-loft fleece to top of eraser. Center stitched design over eraser. Glue fabric edges to sides of eraser, tucking fabric at corners. Let dry.
3. Glue center of rattail cord to fabric edge at center bottom of design. Glue trim around eraser, covering raw fabric edges and rattail cord center. Tie rattail cord ends into a bow around chalk pieces.

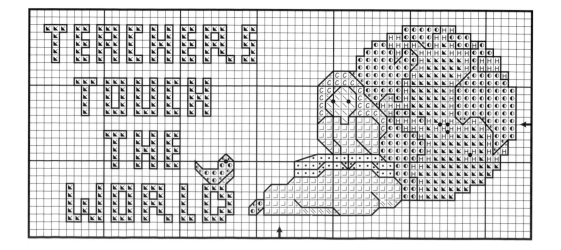

Golf Club Covers

Materials:
Unger Utopia (100-gr./240-yd., worsted-
weight acrylic): 2 skeins dark green
#144 (A); 1 skein light green #142 (B).
One pair size 8 (5.5 mm) knitting needles
Crochet hook size H (5 mm)
Yarn needle
1½" piece of cardboard

Gauge
In St st, 5 sts and 7 rows = 1"

Abbreviations
ch = chain
CO = cast on
dec = decrease
inc = increase
K = knit
P = purl
rem = remaining
rep = repeat
RS = right side
sl st = slipstitch
st(s) = stitch(es)
St st = stockinette stitch (k 1 row, p 1 row)
tog = together
WS = wrong side

Club Cover 1 (one stripe)
With A, CO 38 sts. **Row 1 (RS):** K 2; * p 2, k
2; rep from * across. **Row 2:** P 2; * k 2, p 2;
rep from * across.
Rep rows 1 and 2 for 5", ending after a
WS row.
Dec Row (RS): K 2 tog; * p 2 tog, k 2 tog;
rep from * across—19 sts. **Row 1:** K 1; * p 1,
k 1; rep from * across. **Row 2:** P 1; * k 1, p 1;
rep from * across. **Row 3:** Rep row 1.
Inc Row (RS): Inc 19 sts across by
knitting in front and back of each st—38
sts. P 1 row.
In St st, work 8 more rows A, 3 rows B, 9
rows A.
Dec Row 1: With A, k 2 tog across—19 sts.
Dec Row 2: P 2 tog across to last st, p
1—10 sts.

Finishing
Break yarn leaving a 12" tail. Using yarn
needle, thread tail through rem sts and
draw up tightly to close tip. Sew side seam.

Club Cover 2 (two stripes)
Work as for *Club Cover 1* through Inc
Row. P 1 row.
In St st, work 6 more rows A, 3 rows B, 4
rows A, 3 rows B, 4 rows A. Complete as
for *Club Cover 1.*

Club Cover 3 (three stripes)
Work as for *Club Cover 1* through Inc
Row. P 1 row.
In St st, work (3 rows A, 3 rows B) 3 times,
2 rows A. Complete as for *Club Cover 1.*

Club Cover 4 (four stripes)
Work as for *Club Cover 1* through Inc
Row. P 1 row.

In St st, work (3 rows B, 2 rows A) 4 times.
Complete as for *Club Cover 1.*

Pompoms (make 4)
Holding 1 strand each of A and B, wind
yarn around a 1½" piece of cardboard
about 150 times. At one end, slip one 5"
piece of yarn under loops and knot tightly.
Cut loops at other end. Trim evenly. Attach
one at end of each club cover.

Linking Cord
With crochet hook and 1 strand each A
and B, join with sl st to 1 st in first Dec
Row 1 of club cover 1; * ch 24, sl st in same
row of club cover 2; rep from * for rem 2
club covers. Fasten off.

Sewing Caddy

Materials:
Two 9" x 12" pieces floral cotton fabric (for caddy)
4" x 7" piece coordinating solid fabric (for thimble pouch)
9" x 12" piece coordinating felt (for accessories pockets)
9" x 12" piece batting
⅓yd. Wright's ¾"-wide white scalloped lace trim
1 yd. Wright's 1⅞"-wide white lace trim
2 yds. Wright's ⅛"-wide pink double-face satin ribbon
½yd. Wright's® pink Ribbon Rose Garland
Creative Beginnings brass findings: 1¼" x 3½" frame, 1¾" feather, two 1¼" hearts
Disappearing fabric marker
Threads to match fabrics and felt
Glue gun
Measuring tape
Scissors
Tracing paper
Sewing machine   Pencil

Note: Unless otherwise indicated, all seam allowances are ⅜" and all seams are sewn with right sides facing.

1. Trace patterns onto tracing paper, transferring markings for pin and needle case and cut out. Cut pieces from felt as indicated on patterns.
2. For inside of caddy, baste batting to wrong side of one floral piece. Sew accessories pockets to the right side of this piece as follows, stitching through all layers and referring to Assembly Diagram.
3. To make the thimble pouch, fold fabric in half lengthwise with right sides facing. Sew edges of one short end together. Turn long top edge under ¼" twice to form casing for ribbon; stitch close to lower fold. Stitch edges of remaining short end together up to lower edge of casing. Cut one 14" length from ⅛"-wide satin ribbon and thread through casing. Sew back of caddy to pouch, stitching a vertical line from lower edge of casing to bottom of pouch.
4. For the scissors pockets, cut scalloped lace to fit across top edge of each pocket and sew in place. From satin ribbon, cut one 11" length for small pocket and one 18" length for large pocket. Make a loop with each ribbon length and tack ends to wrong side of top right corner of appropriate pocket. Topstitch each pocket to caddy around outside edges, leaving top edge open.
5. For the thread holder, cut one 16" length from ribbon and center lengthwise on wrong side of holder. Topstitch

holder to caddy, making certain ribbon is centered on ends before stitching.
6. For the ruler pocket, topstitch to caddy, leaving curved end open.
7. To make the pin and needle case, layer pieces, placing piece with cut out area on top. Sew pieces together as indicated on pattern to form needle case. Fold in half and topstitch to caddy, stitching close to fold.
8. Cut 1⅞"-wide lace in half and sew one lace length along each side edge of caddy. Cut one 2" ribbon length and fold in half to make a closing loop. With cut ends of ribbon even with raw edge of fabric, tack loop end to center top edge of caddy. Sew floral caddy pieces together, leaving an opening for turning. Turn and slipstitch opening closed. Topstitch around edges of caddy, ¼" from edge. Refer to photo and glue brass findings and ribbon roses in place. Glue heart charms together. Fold bottom 3" of caddy up, and then fold top 3" down. Mark fabric

inside closing loop to determine position for fastening charm. Glue center of charm to fabric.

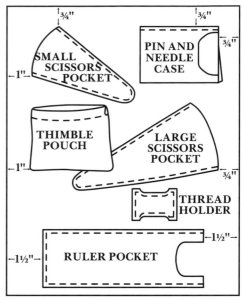

ASSEMBLY DIAGRAM

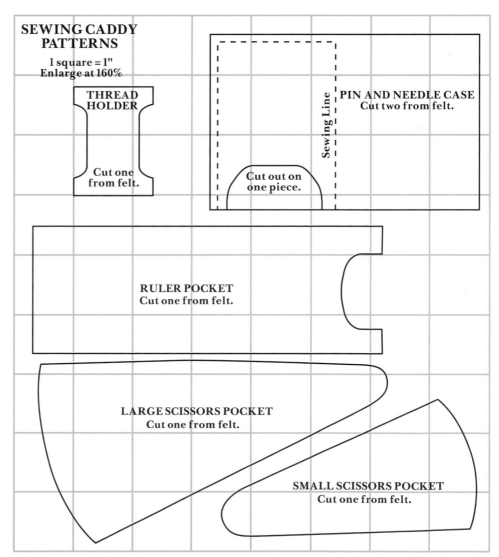

SEWING CADDY PATTERNS
1 square = 1"
Enlarge at 160%

THREAD HOLDER
Cut one from felt.

PIN AND NEEDLE CASE
Cut two from felt.

Sewing Line

Cut out on one piece.

RULER POCKET
Cut one from felt.

LARGE SCISSORS POCKET
Cut one from felt.

SMALL SCISSORS POCKET
Cut one from felt.

Musical Note & Angel Bookmarks

Musical Note Bookmark

Materials:
4" x 8" piece sheet music
Two 5" x 8" sheets Back Street Designs
gold foil scherenschnitte paper
8" x 10" piece transfer fusing web
Clear self-adhesive vinyl
Four skeins dark red embroidery floss
(for tassel)
Gold metallic thread
Pencil
4"-square piece of cardboard
Paper punch
Iron
Scissors
Thick craft glue

1. Use fusing web to fuse gold paper pieces together with wrong sides facing. Following manufacturer's instructions, trace musical note onto fusing web paper and fuse to wrong side of sheet music. Cut out musical note and fuse to gold paper. Cut gold foil ¼" beyond musical note edge.
2. Laminate bookmark between two pieces of clear self-adhesive vinyl. Trim vinyl ⅛" beyond bookmark edge. Punch hole in top of note.
3. To make a twisted cord, cut four 1½-yd. strands of floss and two 1½-yd. strands of gold metallic thread. Knot strands together at one end. Use tape to secure knot to a fixed object. Twist strands together firmly in a clockwise direction until they begin to kink if tension is relaxed. Bring free end to knotted end, folding strands in half, and allow the two halves to twist together. Knot ends to secure. Fold twisted cord in half to form a loop and knot ends. To make the tassel, wrap four strands floss blended with two strands gold metallic thread around cardboard square 24 times.
4. Cut off cardboard along one edge and wrap center of tassel floss strands over twisted cord knot. Place glue on knot and smooth floss strands to form tassel head. Wrap neck of tassel with floss and gold thread to ½", knot to secure, and hide knot under strands.
5. Attach tassel to bookmark through hole at top.

Angel Bookmark

Materials:
Two 2¾" x 6¾" pieces purple taffeta
(for background and backing)
2" x 5" piece pink taffeta (for angel)
2" x 4" piece blue taffeta (for wings)
1" square gold lamé fabric (for halo)
4" x 6" piece transfer fusing web
1 yd. ½"-wide gold flat trim
Four skeins pink embroidery floss
Pink and purple sewing threads
4"-square piece of cardboard
Pencil
Gold metallic thread
Iron
Scissors

1. Trace appliqué patterns onto tracing paper and cut out. Reverse patterns and trace onto paper side of fusing web; cut fusing web apart between motifs. Follow manufacturer's instructions to fuse motifs to wrong side of appropriate fabrics. Cut out motifs on pattern lines and peel away paper backing. Position and then fuse halo, wings, and angel to right side of one purple taffeta piece. Machine satin-stitch angel edges with pink thread and wing and halo edges with gold metallic thread.
2. Sew purple taffeta pieces together with right sides facing, using ¼" seam allowance and leaving an opening for turning. Turn and slipstitch opening closed. Sew gold trim around edge.
3. Follow *Musical Note Bookmark* directions to make twisted cord and tassel with pink floss.
4. Make a small hole in center top edge of bookmark and attach tassel.

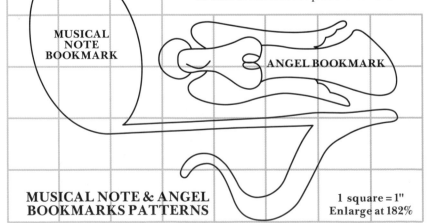

MUSICAL NOTE & ANGEL BOOKMARKS PATTERNS

1 square = 1"
Enlarge at 182%

MUSICAL NOTE BOOKMARK

ANGEL BOOKMARK

Mother's Memory Book

Materials:
Purchased journal, approximately
    5½" x 9"
½yd. 44/45"-wide cotton batiste (for
    foundation and lining)
12" square fleece
Scraps of lace, appliqué, satin, taffeta,
    polished cotton
Assorted novelty threads, floss, beads
1½yds. white narrow piping
½yd. 1"-wide ribbon, cut into 18" lengths
    (for closure ties)
Sewing machine
Threads to match fabrics
Fabric marker
Scissors

1. On batiste fabric, open journal and trace around journal front, width, and back to make one long rectangle for crazy-quilt foundation. Add ⅜" seam allowance and cut out. Cut another piece of batiste the same size for the lining. Cut two batiste pieces, each the height of the journal and 4½" wide, for flaps.

2. To cover batiste foundation piece with crazy-quilt patchwork, cut one 1½"-2" irregularly shaped, four-sided piece of fabric or lace. Pin right-side-up to center of foundation piece. Cut second piece of fabric slightly larger than the first piece. Place right-side-down over first piece, aligning one edge, and sew through all layers. Open second piece and press flat. Repeat to cut and sew pieces in place until foundation fabric is completely covered. Trim patchwork even with foundation edges. (**Note:** Line lace pieces with satin or taffeta and sew as one piece.)

3. Embellish seams with trims, embroidery stitches, and beads as desired, referring to Stitch Illustrations on page **141**.

4. To finish cover, sew piping around edge; trim seam allowance to ¼". Hem one long edge of each batiste flap piece. With right sides facing and raw edges even, sew a flap piece to each end of cover. With right sides facing, sew batiste lining piece to quilted front along top and bottom edges. Trim flap seam allowance to ⅛" and turn.

5. Slipstitch ribbon tie ends to lining at center of each end of cover. Slip cover over journal.

All Around the House

Get set for seasonal giving that's bound to be enjoyed throughout the house the whole year through. Make a hit with your holiday hostess by bringing along a bread-and-butter gift that will charm her. From decorative guest towels to practical refrigerator magnets, there is a perfect something for everyone you'll want to remember this season.

If your friend is a gardener, take along the Garden Wall Quilt or the colorful Sunflower Table Toppers set. Molded Soaps will be a thoughtful present, and you need not worry about size or fit! For a touch of summer in the middle of winter, present the Watermelon Apron to a special cook and include the coordinating mugs and flowerpots. Looking for something to do with those odd buttons in your sewing box? Use them to transform a plain bentwood box into a trinket holder that will be sitting pretty wherever it's placed. Perhaps you prefer stitchery or quilting—this chapter has plenty of that, too!

Watermelon Apron, Mugs, & Flowerpots

Watermelon Apron

Materials:
BagWorks white apron with pocket
DecoArt™ Americana™ acrylic paint, colors: holly green, brilliant red, snow white, lamp black
Paintbrushes, sizes: 4 flat, 1 round
Pencil
Iron-on transfer pencil
Tracing paper
Iron
Yardstick
Art eraser

1. Using yardstick and pencil, lightly draw three rows of ½" checks across top of apron bib. Use flat brush to paint alternating squares with black. Let paint dry and erase remaining pencil lines.
2. Trace watermelon patterns onto tracing paper and cut out ½" beyond traced line. Follow manufacturer's instructions for transfer pencil, and randomly transfer watermelon slices to front of apron.
3. For each watermelon slice, paint rind with green on the outside and white on the inside. Paint red area from edge toward center, letting fabric show through in center for highlight. Let dry.
4. Use round brush to paint seeds with black. Let dry.

Watermelon Mugs & Flowerpots

Materials:
White ceramic mugs
4½" clay flowerpots
Liquitex® Glossies™ oven-bake acrylic enamel paint, colors: red, green, white, black
White spray paint (for pots)
Paintbrushes, sizes: 4, 6, 10 flat; 2 round
Sponge or upholsterer's foam
Disposable palette
Masking tape
Liquid soap
Tracing paper
Pencil
Vinegar
Paper towels

Note: Pieces are dishwasher safe when painted with this brand of acrylic enamels. If using another brand, do not bake or place in dishwasher unless manufacturer indicates otherwise.

1. Wash surfaces to be painted with soap and water. Rinse with a mixture of equal parts water and vinegar to remove any remaining soap film or oils. Let dry. Spray-paint pots with white and let dry.
2. Shake paint bottles well. Pour a small amount of black paint onto palette. Using size 6 brush for mugs and size 10 brush for pots, refer to photo and paint a border of alternating black checks around the top of each piece. Let dry.
3. For pieces with individual watermelon slices, trace patterns, cut out, and cut one of each from sponge or upholsterer's foam. Pour a small amount of red paint onto palette. Dip sponge shape in paint, blot excess on paper towels, and press lightly onto mug or pot. Repeat with both sponge shapes to randomly apply watermelon slices around entire piece. Let dry. To paint watermelon rinds, pour small amounts of white, green, and black paints onto palette. Using size 4 brush, paint a white stripe along curved edge of each watermelon slice. Double-load brush by dipping one corner of brush in white and the other corner in green. Brush back and forth over same place on palette until colors begin to blend together in brush center. With green toward outside, paint over each white stripe, reloading brush as needed. Add a small amount of red to green paint on palette and paint along outside edge of watermelon rinds to darken. Use size 2 brush to paint black seeds on watermelon slices.
4. For each overall watermelon design piece, cover lower edge of checked border with masking tape to protect. Pour small amounts of red and white paints onto palette. Cut one 2" square of sponge or foam and pull up corners to eliminate sharp edges. Dip into white paint and blot on palette to soften color. Dab a row of white around mug or pot directly below border. Dip sponge into red and dab over white paint until colors blend together softly. Continue loading sponge with red and dabbing onto surface to ½" from bottom edge. Randomly paint white highlights on red area, and then soften by sponging lightly over white with red. To paint a rind on each piece, use size 10 brush and paint one ¾"-wide white stripe around bottom edge. Follow step 3 to complete rind and paint seeds.
5. Following manufacturer's instructions, bake painted pieces in oven to make dishwasher safe.

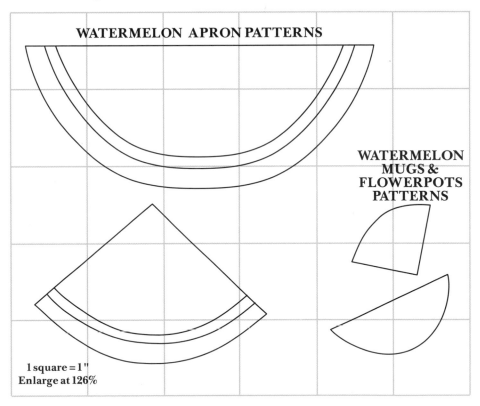

WATERMELON APRON PATTERNS

WATERMELON MUGS & FLOWERPOTS PATTERNS

1 square = 1"
Enlarge at 126%

Kitchen Magnets

Holy Cow

DMC	Color
∕ white	white
■ 310	black
↙ 321	red
↙ 725	yellow, med.
λ 761	pink, pale
bs 702	kelly green

Fabric: 18-count Fiddler's Lite Aida from Charles Craft, Inc.

Stitch count: 39H x 37W
Design size:

11-count	3½" x 3⅜"
14-count	2¾" x 2⅝"
18-count	2⅛" x 2"
22-count	1¾" x 1⅝"

Instructions: Cross stitch using two strands of floss. Backstitch using one strand of floss. Make French knots using one strand of floss, wrapping floss around needle twice.

Backstitch (bs) instructions:

310	cow
321	lettering
702	grass

French knot instructions:

310	cow's eyes

Some Bunny Loves You

DMC	Color
∕ white	white
+ 334	blue, lt.
X 335	rose, dk.
○ 3326	rose, lt.
bs 336	blue, dk.
bs 898	brown, dk.

Fabric: 18-count Fiddler's Lite Aida from Charles Craft, Inc.

Stitch count: 33H x 32W
Design size:

11-count	3" x 3"
14-count	2⅜" x 2¼"
18-count	1⅞" x 1¾"
22-count	1½" x 1½"

Instructions: Cross stitch using two strands of floss. Backstitch using one strand of floss. Make French knots for bunny's eyes, using one strand 898 and wrapping floss around needle twice.

Backstitch (bs) instructions:

336	lettering
898	bunny and bow

Materials:
Pop-in plastic frames with 2½" opening: one **each** red, blue
Two 2¾" circles lightweight cardboard (for backs)
Two 2" lengths self-adhesive magnetic strip
Scissors
White craft glue

1. Complete all cross stitch following instructions given.
2. Center each design in a frame and snap frame pieces together. Trim excess cross stitch fabric even with frame in back.
3. Glue cardboard circle to back of frame. Peel backing from magnetic strip and adhere to center of cardboard back.

Happy Cook Pot Holder

Materials:

¼ yd. 44/45"-wide light print fabric (for dress and backing)

8" square coordinating darker print fabric (for apron)

4" square peach solid fabric (for face and hands)

3" x 4" piece brown fabric (for hair)

1½" x 2½" piece contrasting brown fabric (for shoes)

¾ yd. ¼"-wide ivory lace trim (for apron)

12" square cotton batting

Embroidery floss, colors: red, dark brown, blue

Threads to match fabrics

Clear nylon thread (for quilting)

Hand-sewing needle

Dressmaker's carbon paper

Sewing machine

Embroidery needle

Pencil

Tracing paper

Scissors

⅝" plastic ring

Note: Materials listed will make one *Happy Cook Pot Holder.* All seam allowances are ¼" unless otherwise indicated.

1. Trace around all pattern pieces as indicated. Trace one complete head, dress, and shoe piece **each** from light print backing fabric and batting. Trace remaining pieces on fabrics as indicated on pattern. Trace facial features onto tracing paper. Transfer features lightly to peach solid fabric using dressmaker's carbon. Using one strand of embroidery floss, back-stitch nose and eye outlines with brown and the mouth with red. Using one strand of floss, make blue French knots for eyes. Cut out fabric pieces, adding ¼" seam allowances when cutting each segment.

3. Turn under seam allowance on top edge of face piece and appliqué to hair piece. Turn under seam allowance on apron edges and baste lace around entire piece. Appliqué apron to dress front, catching lace in stitching; remove basting stitches and press. Sew hands to sleeves; turn under outside edges on sleeves and appliqué to dress front. Appliqué bottom of head to top of dress. Sew shoe pieces with right sides facing, leaving straight edge open; clip curves, turn, and press. With raw edges even, sew shoes to center bottom dress edge. Layer batting, backing (right-side-up), then front right-side-down). Sew together, leaving a 3" opening in side for turning. Clip curves; trim backing and batting close to seam. Turn and slipstitch opening closed.

4. Use clear nylon thread to hand- or machine-quilt hair part and bun line, around face, and around apron.

5. Sew plastic ring to top of head.

HAPPY COOK POT HOLDER PATTERN

1 square = 1"
Enlarge at 205%

HAIR
Cut one from brown fabric.

FACE
Cut one from embroidered peach fabric.

ARM
Cut one from light print fabric.

ARM
Cut one from light print fabric.

HANDS
Cut one of each from peach solid fabric.

APRON
Cut one from dark print fabric.

DRESS
Cut one from light print fabric.

SHOES
Cut one from brown fabric.

Note: Dashed lines indicate underlap of pieces.

Cross-Stitch Towels

DMC	Color
♥ 500	blue green, vy. dk.
✖ 501	blue green, dk.
C 503	blue green, med.
H 817	coral red, vy. dk.
• white	white
— 644	beige gray, med.
■ 310	black
★ 327	violet, dk.
◑ 3687	mauve
◕ 312	navy, lt.
⑊ 334	blue, lt.
⌐ 3325	baby blue
∅ 840	beige brown, med.
644	beige gray, med.
+ 841	beige brown, lt.
△ 840	beige brown, med.
✳ 839	beige brown, dk.
▲ 838	brown, dk.
∧ 754	peach flesh, lt.
✕ 350	coral, med.
∽ 352	coral, lt.

Fabric: 14-count ecru (for blue jays), mint green (for hummingbirds), and peach (for robins) Royal Lace Hand Towels from Crafter's Pride

Stitch count:

Blue Jays	30H x 120W
Hummingbirds	30H x 132W
Robins	30H x 110W

Design size:

Blue Jays	14-count	2⅛" x 8⅝"
Hummingbirds	14-count	2⅛" x 9⅜"
Robins	14-count	2⅛" x 7⅞"

Instructions: Cross stitch using two strands of floss. Backstitch using one strand of floss unless otherwise indicated. Straight stitch using two strands of floss. Make French knots using one strand of floss, wrapping floss around needle once. When two colors are bracketed together, use one strand of each.

Backstitch instructions:

838	branches (two strands)
334	baby blue jays in nest
839	nest
310	blue jays, beaks and eyes of hummingbirds, robins
3687	flower stamens in *Hummingbirds*
501	flower stems in *Hummingbirds*
500	remainder of hummingbirds
352	peach blossoms

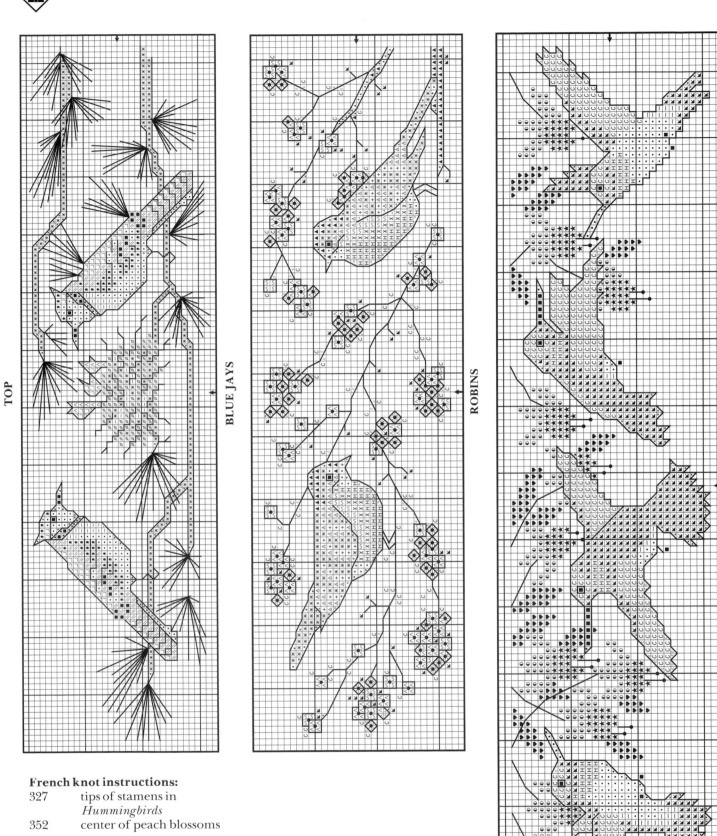

TOP

BLUE JAYS

ROBINS

HUMMINGBIRDS

French knot instructions:

327   tips of stamens in
        Hummingbirds

352   center of peach blossoms

Straight stitch instructions:

500   pine needles (one strand of
503   each)

Button Box & Crazy-Quilt Box

Button Box

Materials:

5½" x 4¼" x 2⅜" oval wood box
¼ yd. 44/45"-wide blue-and-white print fabric
5 to 6 dozen JHB buttons in assorted colors and sizes
9" length 1½"-wide peach gathered lace
1 yd. ¾"-wide white flat Cluny lace
2 yds. ⅛"-wide green satin ribbon
Loctite Creatively Yours Crafter's Cement
Heat and cool glue gun
Hand-sewing needle
Peach sewing thread
Scissors
Tape measure
Pencil

1. Measure around box sides and cut a strip of fabric ½" longer and wider than measurement. Measure around lid sides and cut fabric strip to fit. Place box lid right-side-down on wrong side of fabric, trace around lid edges with pencil, and cut out fabric oval.

2. To cover box, press under a ¹/₁₆" hem along one long edge of fabric for box sides. Apply craft cement to box sides and press on fabric strip, aligning hemmed fabric edge with bottom of box and overlapping fabric edges in back. Let dry and trim fabric even with top edge of box sides. Apply glue to lid and lid sides and press on fabric pieces. Let dry. Cut and glue Cluny lace around lid sides and lower edge of box sides. Cut and glue ribbon around edge of lid sides and lower edge of box sides.

3. Sew a running stitch along bound edge of peach lace, pull tightly to gather into a circle, and knot thread ends. Sew a button to center of lace circle. Tie remaining ribbon into a multi-loop bow with 2½" loops and sew bow center to back of lace circle; hot glue to left side of lid top. Hot glue lace to center of bow. Hot glue buttons to lid.

Crazy-Quilt Box

Materials:

Sudberry House 6"-square black wood box with 5" opening in lid
Scraps of fabric in shades of deep red and burgundy
Old neckties in shades of deep red and burgundy (remove lining and interfacing)
Creative Beginnings charms in assorted styles
JHB buttons in assorted styles
Glass beads in coordinating colors
Embroidery threads of choice: floss, silk buttonhole twist, metallic threads
Braid or trim scraps
Threads to match fabrics
5" square batting
Sewing machine
Plain newsprint paper
5"-square piece tracing paper

Chalk pencil   Scissors
Straight pins

1. Draw a 7" square in the center of one piece of newsprint paper. This will be crazy-quilting foundation.

2. Cover newsprint foundation piece with crazy-quilt patchwork, following instructions on page **49**. Tear away newsprint paper.

3. Center tracing paper square over pieced fabric. Trace around paper edges with chalk pencil, and then baste along chalk line; do not trim excess fabric.

4. Embellish seams with trims, embroidery stitches, and beads as desired. Use matching threads to sew on charms and buttons. Trim finished piece to 5½" square.

5. Follow manufacturer's instructions to insert crazy-quilted piece and batting in wood box lid.

Garden Wall Quilt

Quilt size: 13" x 15"

Materials:
½ yd. 44/45"-wide green print cotton fabric (for binding and backing)
⅛ yd. 44/45"-wide rust print (for border)
⅛ yd. 44/45"-wide gold print (for border corners and flower petals)
10" x 12" piece light tan print cotton fabric (for background)
Scraps of assorted print fabrics (for appliqués)
½ yd. Pellon® Wonder-Under® Transfer Fusing Web
13½" x 15½" piece low-loft quilt batting
Threads to match fabrics
White quilting thread
Hand-sewing needle
Fine-tip permanent black marker
Tape measure
Sewing machine
Straight pins
Iron

Note: Use a ¼" seam allowance and sew all seams with right sides facing unless otherwise indicated.

1. From green print fabric, cut one 13½" x 15½" piece for backing, two 1¾" x 13½" strips for binding top and bottom, and two 2" x 12" strips for binding sides. From rust print, cut two 2" x 10" strips for top and bottom borders and two 2" x 12" strips for side borders. Cut four 2" squares from gold print fabric for border corners. Trace appliqué patterns onto tracing paper and cut out. Reverse patterns and trace onto paper side of fusing web; cut web apart between motifs. Follow manufacturer's instructions to fuse motifs to wrong side of appropriate fabrics. Cut out motifs on pattern lines and peel away paper backing.
Note: Cut each sunflower out as a whole flower rather than cutting individual petals.
2. Sew side border strips to background fabric and press open. Sew border corners to ends of top and bottom border strips. Sew top and bottom strips to background fabric.
3. Referring to photo and pattern, fuse lattice appliqué strips to background fabric. Fuse remaining appliqué pieces in place, positioning underlapping pieces first.
4. Using permanent marker, add bee outline, stripes, and legs; trowel outline, glove outline, and dashed lines; dashed lines on flowerpot and watering can bands; and dashed lines from watering can to flowers.
5. Layer backing (right-side-down), batting, and top (centered right-side-up). Pin layers together securely. Hand-quilt background fabric around all appliqué pieces.
6. Trim batting and backing to ¼" beyond top. With raw edges even, sew binding strips to top and bottom edges of quilt top. Fold binding to back, turn under raw edges, and slipstitch to back. Sew side binding strips to top, turning under raw ends even with top and bottom edges. Fold to back, turn under raw edges, and slipstitch to back.

GARDEN WALL QUILT PATTERN

1 square = 1"   Enlarge at 442%

Note: Dashed lines indicate underlap of pattern pieces.

59

Strip-Quilted
Mitt & Towel

Materials:
⅝ yd. 44/45"-wide unbleached muslin fabric
½ yd. 44/45"-wide blue pindot fabric
¼ yd. **each** five 44/45"-wide coordinating print fabrics
20" x 30" piece high-loft quilt batting
Peach terry cloth hand towel
Sewing machine
Threads to match fabrics
Scissors
Straight pins
Iron
Pencil
Tracing paper

Note: All seams are ¼" and all seams are sewn with right sides facing unless otherwise indicated.

1. Trace patterns onto tracing paper and cut out. From blue pindot, cut one 9" x 20" piece for oven mitt back and two 1¼" x 7" strips and one 1¼" x 30" strip for binding. From muslin, cut one 20" square for oven mitt top and one 9"x 20" piece for back. For strip-quilting, cut 20"-long strips from pindot and print fabrics, varying widths from 1" to 3" to equal 20" wide, excluding ¼" seam allowances. From batting, cut one 20" square for mitt top and one 9" x 20" piece for back.

2. For strip piecing, place batting square on muslin square, aligning edges. Place one fabric strip right side up on batting, aligning raw edges with one edge of batting. Pin a second strip on top of first strip with right sides facing and inside edges even. Sew through all layers along inside edges. Open second strip and press flat. Pin a third strip to second strip with right sides together and inside edges even. Sew seam, open strip, and press flat; repeat, adding strips until muslin square is covered with strip-quilting. From pieced square, cut three hearts, one 2" x 17" strip for hand towel, and one oven mitt top.

3. For mitt back, layer muslin (right-side-down), batting, and blue pindot fabric (right-side-up). Sew diagonal lines across width of fabric, spacing 1" apart and sewing through all layers. Cut one each of oven mitt upper and lower back pattern pieces from quilted piece.

4. To assemble oven mitt, pin upper and lower backs with right sides facing, matching thumb edges. Sew together along thumb seam. Turn and press. Press under ¼" on long edges of bias strips, and then press each strip in half lengthwise to form binding. Sew 7" binding strips over straight edges of top and back mitt pieces. Pin top and back together with wrong sides facing and edges aligned. Turn under raw edges on one end of binding and align with top of one mitt side. Sew binding around edges, making a loop with excess binding at end. Slipstitch binding end to mitt at base of loop.

5. To appliqué towel, pin strip-quilting band across towel, 2" from one end. Trim band ends ¼" longer than towel and press under. Satin stitch edges with blue thread. Refer to photo to pin hearts above band, and then satin stitch edges.

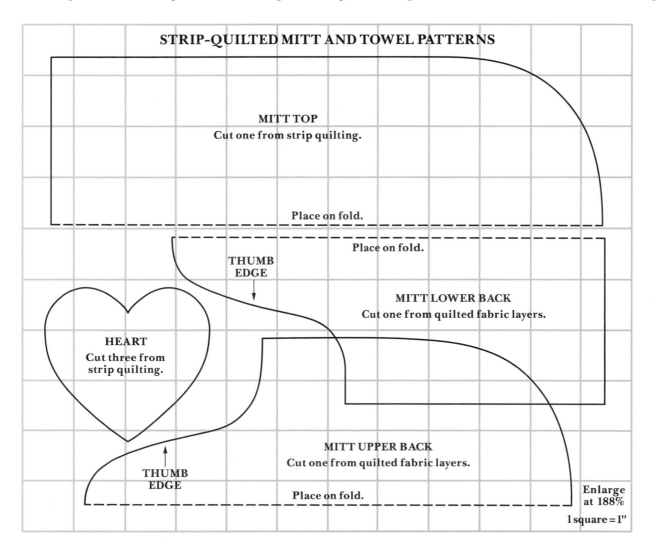

STRIP-QUILTED MITT AND TOWEL PATTERNS

MITT TOP
Cut one from strip quilting.

Place on fold.

Place on fold.

THUMB EDGE

MITT LOWER BACK
Cut one from quilted fabric layers.

HEART
Cut three from strip quilting.

MITT UPPER BACK
Cut one from quilted fabric layers.

THUMB EDGE

Place on fold.

Enlarge at 188%

1 square = 1"

Sunflower Table Toppers

Sunflower Place Mat and Napkin

Materials:

⅓ yd. 44/45"-wide ivory poplin (for
  background and backing)
¼ yd. 44/45"-wide black-and-brown
  print fabric (for binding)
Two 5" x 7" scraps gold print fabrics (for
  flowers)
Two 3" x 4" scraps plaid fabric (for leaves)
Two 2" x 4" scraps brown print fabrics
  (for flower centers)
4" x 6" scrap green print (for stems)
14" square brown print fabric (for
  napkin)
⅔ yd. Pellon® Wonder-Under® Transfer
  Fusing Web
17" x 11½" rectangle fleece
Sewing machine
Threads to match brown and ivory
  fabrics
Disappearing fabric marker
Tracing paper
Scissors   Iron
Ruler   Straight pins

1. From ivory poplin, cut one 16" x10"
rectangle for the place mat front and
one 17" x 11½" rectangle for the back.
From black-and-brown print, cut two 3"
x 45" strips for binding and one 2¾" x
4½" piece for flowerpot.
2. Trace appliqué patterns onto tracing
paper and cut out. Reverse patterns and
trace onto paper side of fusing web; cut
web apart between motifs. Follow
manufacturer's instructions to fuse
motifs to wrong side of appropriate
fabrics. Cut out motifs on pattern lines
and peel away paper backing. Refer to
photo and fuse pieces to place mat
front in following order: stems, leaves,
flowers, and flower centers.
3. Use fabric marker to lightly mark
quilting lines from place mat edges toward center, stopping at appliqué edges.
Draw diagonal lines from corner to
corner, two diagonal lines 5½" from top
corners to 5½" from opposite bottom corners, and a horizontal line across center.
4. Layer backing (right-side-down),
fleece, and front (centered right-side-up).
Pin layers together. Machine-quilt along

quilting lines and around appliqué edges with ivory thread.

5. To make flowerpot, fold fabric in half lengthwise with right sides facing. Using a ¼" seam allowance, sew long edges together; turn. Fold in half to make a loop and baste to base of stems with raw edges of loop and place mat even. Scrunch to shape as desired and slipstitch to stems.

6. Cut ends of binding strips at a 45° angle and sew together to make one long strip. Fold strip in half lengthwise, wrong sides together, and press. With right sides facing and raw edges of top and binding even, sew binding around place mat, mitering corners. Fold binding to back, press under raw edges, and slipstitch in place.

7. For napkin, machine-hem edges of 14" fabric square, mitering corners.

Napkin Ring

Materials:
3"-diameter twig wreath
6" piece wired pine sprig
Small burnt orange and gold dried flowers
1 yd. ⅛"-wide burnt orange satin ribbon
Spool wire
Wirecutters   Hot glue gun

1. Wrap pine sprig around wreath and glue in place. Tie ribbon into a multiloop bow, securing center with wire, and attach to wreath.

2. Break off small pieces of dried flowers and glue into pine sprig.

Sunflower Flag

Materials:
12" x 11" piece ivory trigger fabric
   (for flag)
Two 5" x 7" scraps of gold print fabrics
   (for flowers)
Two 3" x 4" scraps plaid fabric (for leaves)
Two 2" x 4" scraps brown print fabrics
   (for flower centers)
4" x 6" scrap green print (for stems)
1½" x 9½" scrap brown print (for ground)
1½" x 3½" scrap black print (for crow)
⅔ yd. Pellon® Wonder-Under® Transfer
   Fusing Web
1½ yd. 1"-wide Pellon® Wonder-Under®
   Transfer Fusing Web tape
20" length ¼"-diameter dowel rod
Fine-tip permanent black marker
Disappearing fabric marker
Thick craft glue   Tracing paper

Pencil   Window or light box
Masking tape   Fabric paint
Scissors   Iron
Gold acrylic paint

1. Follow manufacturer's instructions to fuse 1"-wide fusing tape around outside edges on wrong side of trigger fabric. With fabric right-side-up, make a ½" diagonal cut in right top and bottom corners to miter. Turn under and press ½" along top, bottom, and right edges. To make hanging tabs on left side of flag, use disappearing marker to mark cutting lines on wrong side of fabric (see Illustration). Fuse fusing web tape over marked lines and cut out. Fold tabs to back and fuse in place with fusing web tape, leaving an opening in each tab for dowel rod.

2. Trace appliqué patterns onto tracing paper and cut out. Reverse patterns and trace onto paper side of transfer web; cut web apart between motifs. Follow manufacturer's instructions to fuse motifs to wrong side of appropriate fabrics.

Cut out motifs on pattern lines and remove paper backing. Refer to photo and fuse to flag in following order: stems, ground, leaves, flowers, flower centers, and crow.

3. Write the word "Sunflowers" onto tracing paper and tape to window or light box. Place flag over traced letters and use permanent marker to write letters on fabric.

4. Paint dowel rod gold and let dry. Insert through hanging tabs and glue to secure.

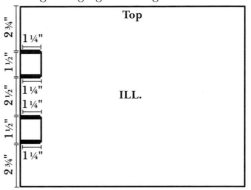

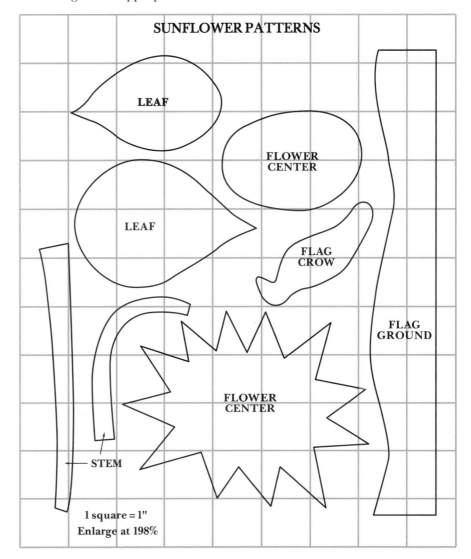

Embroidered Fingertip Towel
& Molded Soaps

Embroidered Fingertip Towel

Materials:
Blue fingertip towel
1⅓ yds. Capitol Imports ⅝"-wide white flat lace (cut into 12" lengths)
⅔yd. Capitol Imports ¾"-wide white Swiss embroidery flat insertion lace (cut into 12" lengths)
1 yd. ⅜"-wide lavender satin ribbon (cut into 12" lengths)
4" square Pellon® Stitch-n-Tear®
Small sharp-pointed scissors
Fabric glue   Iron
Pencil   Straight pins

1. To assemble each lace panel, press long edges of embroidered insertion lace under ⅛". Use fabric glue to glue straight edges of ⅝"-wide lace to pressed-under edges. Weave satin ribbon through eyelets in center of insertion lace. Pin one lace panel across each end of towel, 1½" from end of towel (excluding fringe). Use two strands of dark violet floss (Anchor 111) and sew lace to towel, sewing through holes along edges of insertion lace. Use one strand of white floss to tack outside edges of lace to towel. Turn ends of lace panels to back of towel. Open seams of side towel binding and insert lace ends, trimming ends to fit. Slipstitch seams closed.
2. Trace embroidery pattern onto Stitch-n-Tear paper. Center and pin to one end of towel with flower stems over lace panel. Embroider all flowers and leaves except stems at bottom as indicated. Use small sharp-pointed scissors to trim paper away from design. Refer to the photo and embroider stems.
3. Tie a bow with remaining satin ribbon and sew to towel over stems; trim ribbon ends.

Anchor®	DMC	Color
111	208	violet, dk.
110	209	violet, med.
108	210	violet, lt.
001	white	white
297	973	yellow
246	986	green, dk.
216	367	green, med.
215	320	green, lt.

Note: Models were stitched using Anchor® embroidery floss.
Instructions: Make stitches using two strands of floss and following natural direction of petals and leaves. Make French knots using two strands of floss, wrapping floss around needle once.

Split stitch instructions:
246   leaf edges of violets, leaf outlines and veins of lilies of the valley and stems from bells to violets and back to bells
215   leaf veins of violets
111   petal edges and veins of violets
001   bell edges of lilies of the valley

Satin stitch instructions:
246   leaves of violets (bring stitches over split stitch edge), underside of leaf of lily of the valley on right

216   leaves of lilies of the valley
110   bud and shaded areas on violets
108   petals of violets
001   bells of lilies of the valley (bring stitches over split stitch edge)

Straight stitch instructions:
297   stamens on bells of lilies of the valley

French knot instructions:
297   centers of violets and ends of stamens of lilies of the valley

☐ **Shaded Area**

EMBROIDERED FINGERTIP TOWEL PATTERN (FULL SIZE)

Molded Soaps

Materials:
3- to 4-oz. bar of pure glycerin soap in color and scent of choice
Flexible plastic or rubber candy mold
Microwave-safe glass measuring cup with pouring spout
Craft knife   Spoon

1. Cut bar of soap into ½"-square pieces and place in measuring cup. Microwave on high for 30 to 45 seconds, or until all pieces have melted. **Note:** Do not let soap boil. Stir melted soap if necessary, stirring slowly to avoid creating air bubbles.

2. Pour melted soap into molds until level with top of mold. Tap lightly on table to raise any air bubbles to the surface. Refrigerate molds for one hour or until soap is hardened. Bend molds slightly to release shape, tap on table, and remove soap.
3. Let soaps air-dry for at least one week. If moisture forms on soaps during drying period, do not touch, but allow to evaporate.

Holiday Trimmings

A popular tradition among friends is the sharing of yuletide decorating ideas. On the pages that follow are ideas for table toppers, tiny totes, and timeless treasures you can make that will please the lucky recipients and continue to be enjoyed year after year. Choose your favorites for cherished friends this holiday season and expect to hear "oohs" and "aahs" as they discover the hidden wonders in their stockings this Christmas!

Decorative Windowsill Trees are guaranteed to get a second look. If that someone special adores angels, herald the season with a charming trio of handmade beauties, or try your hand at the Angel Wall Hanging, which will change a plain wall into a visual showcase.

Whether your friends' decorating needs include setting a gorgeous table or decking the halls, they're certain to love the gifts you share.

Santa Table Set

Materials:
⅞ yd. 44/45"-wide light color Christmas print fabric
⅞ yd. 44/45"-wide white cotton lining fabric
⅓ yd. 44/45"-wide red solid fabric
½ yd. 44/45"-wide white solid cotton fabric
¼ yd. 44/45"-wide peach solid fabric
10" x 12" piece **each** of black solid and dark pink solid fabrics
1 yd. Pellon® Heavy Duty Wonder-Under® Transfer Fusing Web
2 yds. 22"-wide Pellon® fusible interfacing
½yd. 44/45"-wide white Pellon® fusible fleece
⅓yd. quilt fleece
White maxi piping (for tea cozy and coaster)
Embroidery floss, colors: red, tan (for coaster)
Sewing machine
Threads to match fabrics
Scissors
Tracing paper
Pencil   Iron

Note: Materials listed will make one each of the table runner, tea cozy, and coaster. All seam allowances are ¼" and all seams are sewn with right sides facing unless otherwise indicated.

1. Enlarge patterns as indicated. Cut one 12½" x 31¾" strip **each** from Christmas print fabric, white lining fabric, and fusible fleece for table runner. Trace tea cozy, Santa hat and pom-pom, and oval coaster outline patterns and cut out; cut these pieces from fabrics as indicated on patterns.

2. Fuse interfacing to wrong side of peach, red, dark pink, white cotton, and black fabrics. Trace remaining patterns onto tracing paper and cut out. Reverse patterns and trace onto paper side of fusing web; cut web apart between motifs. Follow manufacturer's instructions to fuse motifs to wrong side of interfaced fabrics as indicated on patterns. Cut out motifs on pattern lines but do not remove paper backing until ready to fuse pieces. Transfer dashed detail lines.

3. **To make the table runner**, layer fusible fleece strip and Christmas print strip with right sides up, aligning edges. Mark center of print fabric strip. For **each** end of the runner, refer to Illustration and pattern markings to position appliqué pieces. Position hat piece on runner with top hat edge 9¾" from runner center. Fuse hat to fabric, being careful not to fuse fabric to fleece below bottom hat edge. Fuse fleece hat pom-pom in place, and then fuse fabric hat pom-pom on top of fleece. Measure ½" below bottom edge of hat and carefully cut away Christmas print fabric, leaving fleece only on end of runner. Layer and fuse remaining pieces to fleece in following order: face, beard, hat trim, mouth, mustache, glasses, nose, eyebrows, eyes, and eye pupils. Trim edges of runner end even with outside edges of Santa head as shown in Illustration.

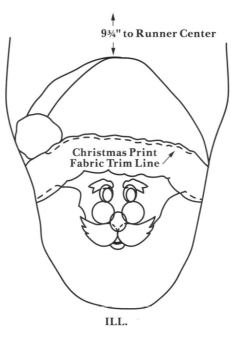

↑
9¾" to Runner Center
↓

Christmas Print Fabric Trim Line

ILL.

4. To finish table runner, sew appliquéd runner front and lining fabric together around edges of front, leaving an opening for turning. Trim excess fabric, turn, and slipstitch opening closed. Use matching threads to machine satin-stitch edges of appliquéd pieces and detail lines on beard and eyeglasses. Satin-stitch black line on mouth.

5. **To make the tea cozy**, cut away seam allowance on tea cozy batting pieces. Fuse front background appliqués to bottom right and left corners of one batting piece. Following instructions for the *table runner*, fuse Santa head appliqué pieces in place and satin-stitch edges and detail lines. Cut away seam allowance on hat interfacing pieces. Center and fuse interfacing to wrong side of each fabric hat piece. Sew hat pieces together along side edges. Turn and press. Sew pom-pom pieces together, leaving an opening for turning. Turn, insert fleece, and slipstitch opening closed. Sew pom-pom to top of hat. Baste hat to top of head with raw edges even. With raw edges toward outside, baste piping around edges of front, beginning and ending at hat edges.

6. Adhere fusing web to wrong side of tea cozy back and fuse to remaining batting piece. With raw edges toward outside, baste piping along bottom edge of back on right side. Sew front and back together, leaving bottom edges open. Turn. Sew lining pieces together, leaving bottom edges open and a 3" opening in top for turning; do not turn. Place tea cozy inside lining with right sides facing and side seams aligned. Sew together along bottom edges. Pull tea cozy through opening in top of lining. Slipstitch opening closed and insert lining in tea cozy. Tack lining to cozy along seam line. Fold hat tip down and tack pom-pom to head.

7. **To make the coaster front**, fuse interfacing to batting oval, and then fuse appliqué pieces to interfacing following *table runner* instructions. Machine satin-stitch all edges and detail lines except eyeglasses. Refer to Stitch Illustrations on page **141** to work remaining stitches by hand. Satin-stitch pupils with black floss and mouth with red floss. Work a chain stitch for outlines and arms of eyeglasses. With raw edges toward outside, baste piping around edges of appliquéd front, beginning and ending at bottom edge.

8. Sew front to back, leaving opening for turning. Turn and slipstitch opening closed.

SANTA TABLE SET PATTERNS

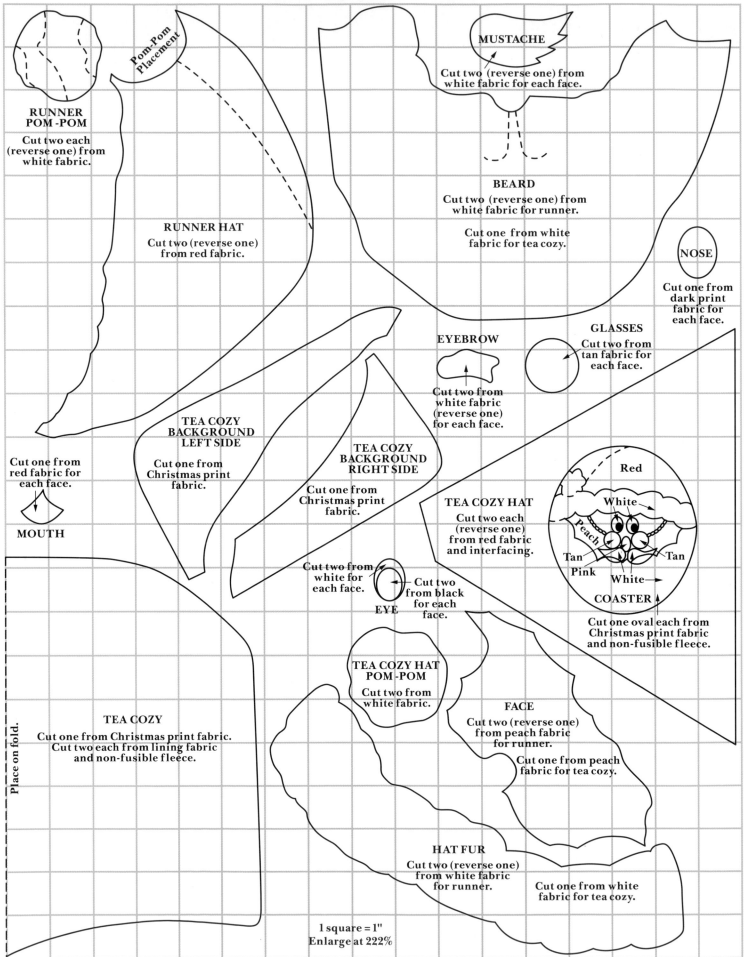

RUNNER POM-POM

Cut two each (reverse one) from white fabric.

Pom-Pom Placement

RUNNER HAT

Cut two (reverse one) from red fabric.

MUSTACHE

Cut two (reverse one) from white fabric for each face.

BEARD

Cut two (reverse one) from white fabric for runner.

Cut one from white fabric for tea cozy.

NOSE

Cut one from dark print fabric for each face.

EYEBROW

Cut two from white fabric (reverse one) for each face.

GLASSES

Cut two from tan fabric for each face.

Cut one from red fabric for each face.

MOUTH

TEA COZY BACKGROUND LEFT SIDE

Cut one from Christmas print fabric.

TEA COZY BACKGROUND RIGHT SIDE

Cut one from Christmas print fabric.

TEA COZY HAT

Cut two each (reverse one) from red fabric and interfacing.

Red
White
Peach
Tan
Pink
Tan
White

COASTER

Cut one oval each from Christmas print fabric and non-fusible fleece.

Cut two from white for each face.

Cut two from black for each face.

EYE

Place on fold.

TEA COZY

Cut one from Christmas print fabric.
Cut two each from lining fabric and non-fusible fleece.

TEA COZY HAT POM-POM

Cut two from white fabric.

FACE

Cut two (reverse one) from peach fabric for runner.

Cut one from peach fabric for tea cozy.

HAT FUR

Cut two (reverse one) from white fabric for runner.

Cut one from white fabric for tea cozy.

1 square = 1"
Enlarge at 222%

70

Stocking Pin

Materials:

Felt scraps: 3" x 6" red, 2" square green,
  1" x 2" white
Embroidery floss, colors: red, green,
  white
6" square Pellon® Wonder-Under®
  Transfer Fusing Web
6" length ¹⁄₁₆"-wide gold braid
1" bar pin back
Tapestry needle
Scissors
Iron
Tracing paper

1. Trace stocking lining pattern onto tracing paper and cut out. Cut one stocking lining from fleece. Trace remaining patterns onto tracing paper and cut out. Reverse patterns and trace onto paper side of fusing web; cut web apart between motifs. Follow manufacturer's instructions to fuse motifs to wrong side of interfaced fabrics as indicated on patterns. Cut out motifs on pattern lines but do not remove paper backing until ready to fuse pieces.

2. Referring to photo, fuse toe, heel, and cuff to one red stocking piece. Fuse leaves to cuff. Work buttonhole stitches around toe, heel, and leaves using one strand of green floss.

3. Place appliquéd stocking front and plain back together with wrong sides facing. Work buttonhole stitch around stocking, using one strand of white floss for cuff and one strand of red floss for remaining areas. Thread tapestry needle with gold braid and stitch through top right corner of stocking. Tie braid into a bow.

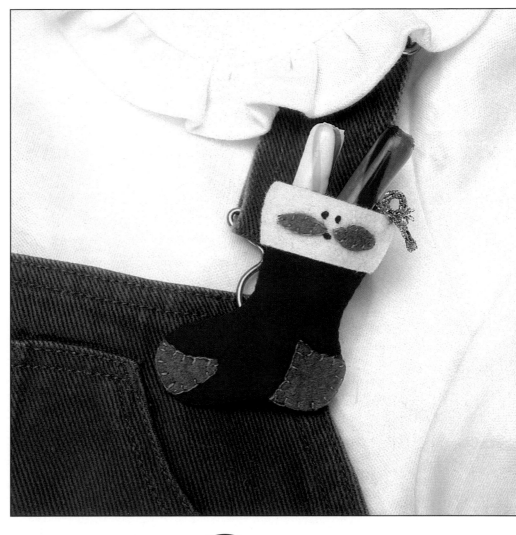

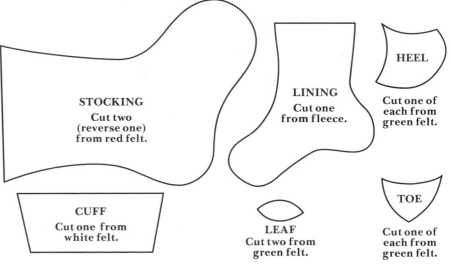

STOCKING
Cut two
(reverse one)
from red felt.

LINING
Cut one
from fleece.

HEEL
Cut one of
each from
green felt.

CUFF
Cut one from
white felt.

LEAF
Cut two from
green felt.

TOE
Cut one of
each from
green felt.

STOCKING PIN PATTERNS (FULL SIZE)

Angel Wall Hanging

Quilt size: 29" x 29"

Materials:

¾ yd. 44/45"-wide Christmas calico fabric (for background and sashing corners)

½ yd. 44/45"-wide red-and-white striped fabric (for sashing and sashing heart appliqués)

1 yd. 44/45"-wide red fabric (for backing)

¼ yd. 44/45"-wide muslin (for wings and faces)

12" square **each** of four different Christmas prints (for appliqués)

6" square **each** of four different Christmas prints (for appliqués)

34" x 40" piece traditional-loft quilt batting

1½ yds. Therm O Web HeatnBond™ Lite 17"-wide iron-on adhesive

16" length Therm O Web HeatnBond™ Lite ⅜"-wide iron-on adhesive tape

1½ yds. ⅜"-wide red satin ribbon

6" length ⅛"-wide red satin ribbon (cut into 3" lengths)

20" length 1/16"-wide red satin ribbon (cut into 5" lengths)

2¾ yd. ¾"-wide ecru gathered cluny lace

1 yd. ½"-wide ecru flat trim

Embroidery floss, colors: red, dark brown

One package auburn synthetic curly hair

Three 1¼" plastic rings (for hanging)

Red and ecru quilting threads

Threads to match fabrics

Small amount polyester fiberfill

Scissors

Straight pins

Iron

Powder blush makeup

Tracing paper

Pencil

Sewing machine

Note: All seam allowances are ¼" and all seams are sewn with right sides facing unless otherwise indicated.

1. Trace wing and stuffed heart patterns onto tracing paper, transferring markings. Cut out, and then cut from fabrics as indicated on patterns. Trace remaining patterns onto tracing paper and cut out. Reverse patterns and trace onto paper side of 17"-wide iron-on adhesive; cut adhesive apart between motifs. Follow manufacturer's instructions to fuse motifs to wrong side of fabrics as indicated on patterns. Cut out motifs on pattern lines and peel away paper. From background fabric, cut four 12" squares for background and nine 2½" squares for sashing strip corners. From red-and-white striped fabric, cut twelve 2½" x 12" strips for sashing. From muslin, cut two 2½" circles for heads and one 34" square. From batting, cut two 10" x 6" rectangles and one 34" square.

2. To make each angel appliqué, center and pin one pair of wings with right sides facing on one 10" x 6" batting piece. Sew around wing edges through all layers. Trim batting even with edges. Cut one 2" slit in center of one wing and turn. Press wing and slipstitch opening closed. Use red quilting thread to hand-quilt around wing ¼" from edge. Center wings on one background square with top of wings 1½" from top edge of square. Sew a vertical line down center of wings to sew to square. Position dress on square with lower edge of dress 1½" from bottom of square. Cut one 11½" length of gathered lace and insert bound edge under bottom edge of dress. Fuse dress in place. Fuse apron in place, adding flat lace under edges before pressing. Fuse sleeves and lower half of head in place. Insert a small piece of batting under head

and complete fusing. Satin-stitch face edge with ecru thread and dress, sleeve, and apron edges with red thread. Referring to photo for placement, make French knots for eyes with dark brown floss and one French knot for mouth with red floss. Apply a small amount of powder blush makeup to cheeks.

3. To make each heart square, position heart top and bottom pieces with edges aligned in center of one background square. Cut gathered lace to fit along straight center edge and around outside edge of heart. Insert lace edge under fabric edge and fuse in place. Cut one 16" length from ⅜"-wide satin ribbon, and using the ⅜"-wide iron-on adhesive, fuse ribbon length along straight edge of upper heart. Using red thread, machine-straight-stitch along ribbon edges and satin-stitch around heart edge. Cut one 14" length from ⅜"-wide ribbon and tie into a bow. Tack to heart as indicated on pattern.

4. Fuse one small heart to center of each 2½" square for sashing corners. Referring to the Assembly Diagram, assemble and sew each sashing row and each quilt block row, and then sew rows together. Press all seams toward darker fabric.

ASSEMBLY DIAGRAM

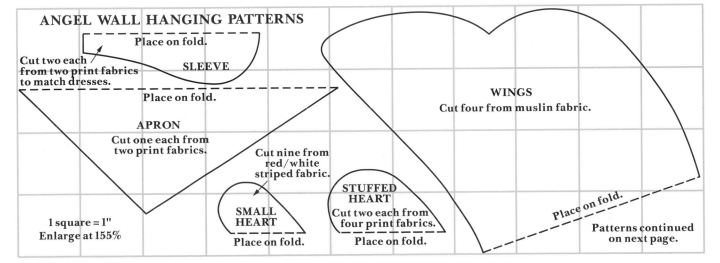

ANGEL WALL HANGING PATTERNS

Place on fold.

Cut two each from two print fabrics to match dresses.

SLEEVE

Place on fold.

APRON
Cut one each from two print fabrics.

1 square = 1"
Enlarge at 155%

Cut nine from red/white striped fabric.

SMALL HEART
Place on fold.

STUFFED HEART
Cut two each from four print fabrics.
Place on fold.

WINGS
Cut four from muslin fabric.

Place on fold.

Patterns continued on next page.

5. Layer 34" muslin square, 34" batting square, and pieced top. Quilt around large hearts, angel skirts, and tops of heads, and quilt in-the-ditch around center square and 12" squares. Trim batting and muslin even with edges of top. Cut one square from red backing fabric the same size as pieced top and place on top with right sides facing. Sew together along edges, leaving an opening for turning. Clip corners and turn. Press and slipstitch opening closed.

6. To make stuffed hearts, pin four pairs of hearts together with right sides facing. Sew each pair together using a ⅛" seam allowance and leaving an opening for turning. Turn and stuff each heart firmly with fiberfill; slipstitch openings closed. Tie each 1/16"-wide ribbon length into a bow and tack one to center of each heart. Sew hearts to ends of ⅛"-wide ribbon lengths. For each angel, sew one stuffed heart over sleeve ends, letting other heart dangle.

7. Cut and hand-sew synthetic hair to each angel's head.

8. Evenly space and sew rings to top back edge of quilt for hanging.

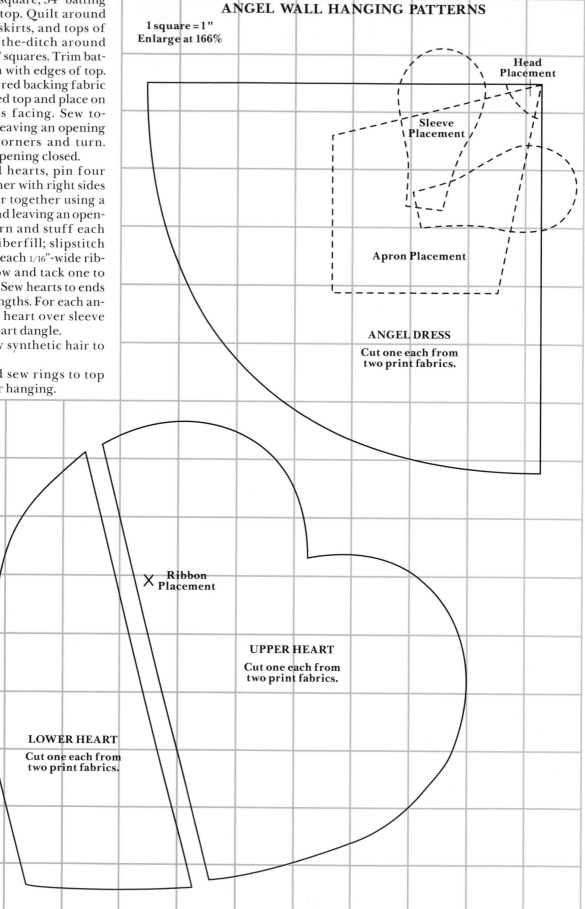

ANGEL WALL HANGING PATTERNS

1 square = 1"
Enlarge at 166%

Head Placement

Sleeve Placement

Apron Placement

ANGEL DRESS

Cut one each from two print fabrics.

X Ribbon Placement

UPPER HEART

Cut one each from two print fabrics.

LOWER HEART

Cut one each from two print fabrics.

"Charming" Christmas Tree

Materials:
10" square tan tightly woven cotton
   fabric (for block center)
10½" square deep red plaid cotton
   fabric (for borders and backing)
Embroidery floss, colors: blue green,
   vy. dk.; gold; dark red; ecru
Kreinik blending filament, color: 32
   pearl
Igolochkoy™ three-strand
   punchneedle
12 Birdhouse Enterprises brass
   Christmas charms
7" square quilt batting
½" plastic ring
Iron-on transfer pencil
Embroidery scissors
5" or 6" embroidery hoop with lip
Measuring tape
Hand-sewing needle
Threads to match fabrics
Tissue paper
Sewing scissors
Iron   Straight pins
Pencil
Clothes dryer

1. Trace tree pattern onto tissue paper using iron-on transfer pencil. Center and transfer design to wrong side of tan fabric square. Place fabric in embroidery hoop with design centered and stretch taut.

2. To punch design, follow manufacturer's instructions and punch areas from wrong side of fabric to form loops on right side, unless reverse punch is indicated. To reverse-punch, hold fabric up to light and use a pencil to lightly sketch design area on right side of fabric. Punch from right side, leaving most of loop on wrong side of fabric. Outline each color area and then fill in, using small stitches and leaving a small amount of space between rows. To begin, punch garland with needle set at ⅜" from eye to gauge and threaded with one strand ecru and two strands blending filament. Set needle at ¼" from eye to gauge, thread with two strands blue green, and punch tree. Reverse-punch candles with dark red and flames with gold. To finish, clip any loose thread ends on front or back of fabric at level of loop. (Knotting is not necessary as the tight weave of the fabric will hold stitches in place). Rinse

design in cool water to remove transfer pencil. Fluff design by drying partially in clothes dryer.

3. To attach each charm, thread needle with dark red floss and make a small stitch through tree and fabric with ends in front. Tie on charm and tie floss into a bow; trim ends. Refer to photo for charm placement.

4. With design centered, trim tan fabric to 7" square. Press under ¼" and then 1" on all edges of red plaid backing fabric. Layer backing fabric (right-side-down), batting (centered), and tan fabric (centered right-side-up). Pin layers together. Bring side edges of backing fabric to front and slipstitch in place. Repeat for top and bottom edges of backing fabric.

5. Hand-sew plastic ring to top back edge of mini-quilt for hanger.

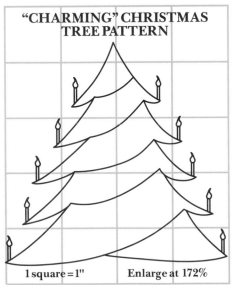

"CHARMING" CHRISTMAS TREE PATTERN

1 square = 1"   Enlarge at 172%

Painted Nutcrackers

Large Nutcracker King

Materials:
Zim's 5½" wood King Nutcracker
DecoArt™ Americana™ acrylic paint, colors: flesh, black, white, burnt umber, Williamsburg blue, burgundy wine
DecoArt™ Dazzling Metallics™ acrylic paint, colors: teal green, glorious gold
Paintbrushes, sizes: 4 flat, 5 round, 1 liner
Waterbase satin varnish
Tracing paper
Chalk pencil
Pencil

1. Using flat brush, base-coat head and hands of nutcracker with flesh and crown top, coat, pants, and top of base with burgundy wine. Paint boots with black.
2. Trace eye pattern and transfer to face with chalk pencil. Paint eyes with white, irises with Williamsburg blue, and pupils with black; let dry and add white highlights to irises and pupils. Mix burgundy wine with a small amount of white to lighten, dip corner of damp flat brush into mixture, and paint cheeks with dark color toward the outside. Paint mustache, eyebrows, and hair with burnt umber. Thin burnt umber and shade above eyes. Using liner brush, outline eyes with black and add detail lines to hair.
3. Referring to photo, use chalk pencil to draw lapel outlines on top of coat and scalloped border around bottom of coat. Paint lapels, bottom border, mouth handle, bands on arms, hat brim, and ball on top with two coats of teal green, letting dry between coats. With glorious gold, paint coat and boot details, belt, top of arms, crown, hat brim dots, and edge of base. Let paint dry thoroughly.
4. Apply an even coat of varnish to nutcracker. Let dry.

Small Nutcracker King

Materials:
Zim's 4⅞" wood King Nutcracker
DecoArt™ Americana™ acrylic paint, colors: flesh, black, white, teal green, burnt umber, Williamsburg blue, burgundy wine
DecoArt™ Dazzling Metallics™ acrylic paint, colors: royal ruby, glorious gold
Paintbrushes, sizes: 4 flat, 5 round, 1 liner
Waterbase satin varnish
Tracing paper
Chalk pencil
Pencil

1. Using flat brush, base-coat head of nutcracker with flesh and crown top and brim, bottom of coat, sleeves and hands, and top of base with teal green. Mix teal green with white and paint coat top, mouth handle, and pants. Paint the boots with black.
2. Trace eye pattern and transfer to face with chalk pencil. Paint eyes with white, irises with Williamsburg blue, and pupils with black; let dry and add white highlights to irises and pupils. Mix burgundy wine with a small amount of white to lighten, dip corner of damp flat brush into mixture, and paint cheeks with dark color toward the outside. Paint mustache, eyebrows, and hair with burnt umber. Using liner brush, outline eyes with black and add detail lines to hair.
3. Referring to photo, paint arm bands, decorative lines on coat, dots on hat brim, and ball on top with royal ruby. With glorious gold, paint dots on coat and arm bands, crown, top line and dots on boots, and edge of base. Let paint dry thoroughly.
4. Apply an even coat of varnish to nutcracker. Let dry.

Nutcracker with Top Hat

Materials:
Zim's 4" wood Nutcracker with Top Hat
Delta Ceramcoat® acrylic paint, colors: flesh, black, white, burnt umber, woodland night, gypsy rose, Cape Cod
DecoArt™ Dazzling Metallics™ acrylic paint, color: glorious gold
Paintbrushes, sizes: 4 flat, 5 round, 1 liner
Waterbase satin varnish
Tracing paper
Chalk pencil
Pencil

1. Using flat brush, base-coat head of nutcracker with flesh and the hat, top of arms, hands, pants, and top of base with woodland night. Mix woodland night with white and paint coat, mouth handle, and sleeves.
2. Trace eye pattern and transfer to face with chalk pencil. Paint eyes with white, irises with Cape Cod, and pupils with black; let dry and add white highlights to irises and pupils. Dip corner of damp flat brush into gypsy rose, and paint cheeks with color toward the outside. Paint mustache, eyebrows, and hair with burnt umber. Using liner brush, outline eyes with black and add detail lines to hair.
3. Referring to photo, paint decorative lines on coat and hat and dots on sleeves with gypsy rose. With glorious gold, paint hat top, hat and sleeve detail lines and dots, and edge of base. Let paint dry thoroughly.
4. Apply an even coat of varnish to nutcracker. Let dry.

— Large Nutcracker King Eye

— Top Hat Nutcracker Eye

— Small Nutcracker King Eye

NUTCRACKER EYE PATTERNS (FULL SIZE)

Button Cross-Stitch Ornaments

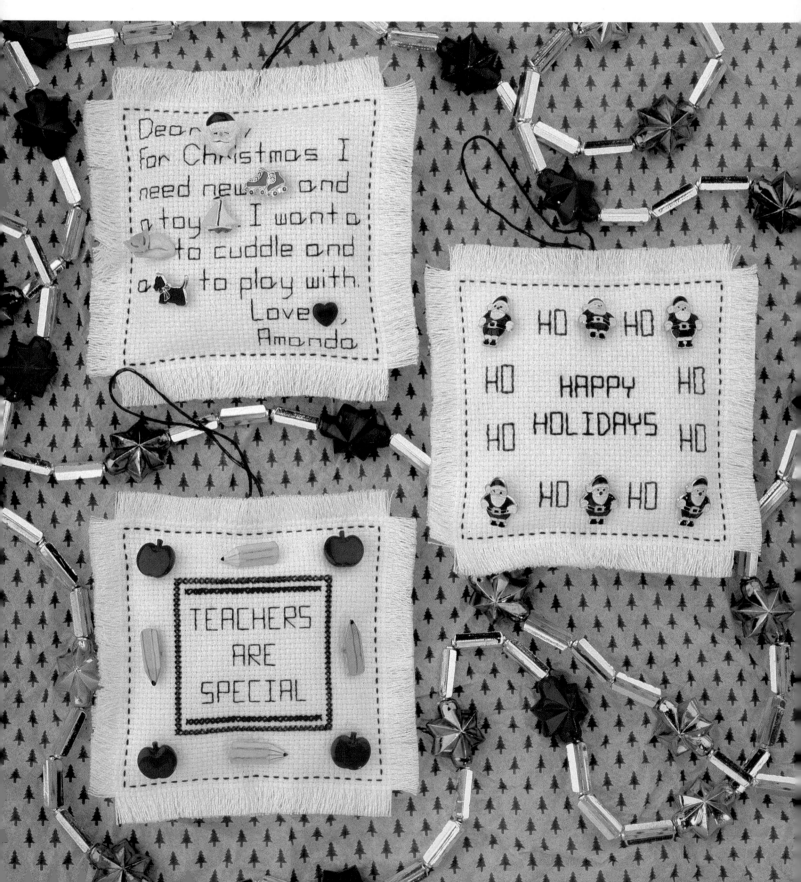

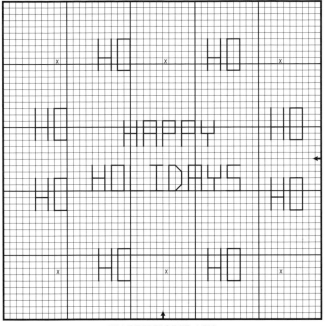

HAPPY HOLIDAYS

DEAR SANTA

	DMC	Color
X	321	red
·	699	green
bs	3371	black-brown

Fabric: 14-count white Aida from Charles Craft, Inc. (Cut fabric for each ornament 6" x 6".)
Stitch count: 50H x 50W

Design size:
11-count	4½" x 4½"
14-count	3⅝" x 3⅝"
18-count	2¾" x 2¾"
22-count	2¼" x 2¼"

Instructions: Cross stitch using two strands of floss. Backstitch using one strand of floss.
Backstitch (bs) instructions:
321	*Happy Holidays*
699	*Ho Ho Ho*
3371	*Teacher, Dear Santa*

Materials:
6" square Aida for **each** ornament (for backing)
JHB buttons: *Happy Holidays* ornament: six Santas; *Teacher* ornament: four pencils, four apples; *Dear Santa* ornament: one each of Santa head, roller skates, sailboat, sleeping kitten, puppy, red heart
Scissors
Polyester fiberfill
White sewing thread

1. Complete all cross stitch following instructions given.

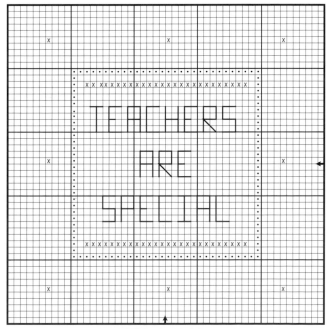

TEACHERS ARE SPECIAL

2. Refer to photo and chart and use sewing thread to sew buttons in place.
3. Place stitched fronts right-side-up over backing pieces, aligning edges. Stitch squares together along edges of three sides using two strands of red floss and running stitch. Stuff with fiberfill and use running stitch and red floss to stitch open side closed. Trim fabric ½" beyond running stitch. Remove threads to make fringe.
4. For each hanger, cut four 7"-long strands of red floss and use to stitch through center of top back ornament edge. Knot ends together to make a loop.

Santa Kaleidoscope

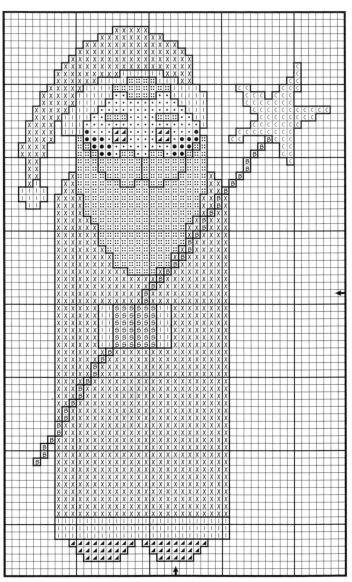

SANTA KALEIDOSCOPE

DMC	DMC Flower Thread (FT)	Color
▲ 310		black
· 754		peach flesh, lt.
● 760		pink
X	2346	red, dk.
∷	2415	pearl gray
B	2610	drab brown, vy. dk.
S	2909	emerald, vy. dk.
I	white	white
C 282	Metallic	lt. gold

Fabric: 14-count white Aida from Charles Craft, Inc.

Stitch count: 73H x 43W
Design size: 14-count 5¼" x 3⅛"
Instructions: Cross stitch using two strands floss, one strand flower thread (FT), or three strands of metallic thread. Backstitch using one strand 310.

Materials:
Home Crafted Toys™ stitcher's kaleidoscope
24" length gold metallic wire star garland
Scissors
1. Complete all cross stitch following instructions given.

2. Cut one 6" length from star garland and set aside. From remaining garland, cut 25 stars and place in kaleidoscope viewing cup.
3. Following manufacturer's instructions, insert stitched design in barrel and assemble kaleidoscope.
4. Wrap 6" garland length around barrel at base of viewing cup, twisting ends together to secure.

Windowsill Trees

Materials:

1" x 12" x 18" sheet Styrofoam® brand plastic foam

⅛ yd. **each** 44/45"-wide light green solid, medium green solid, dark green solid fabrics

¼ yd. 44/45"-wide holiday print fabric

1½ yds. ⅞"-wide dark green grosgrain ribbon

Three ⅝" gold star buttons

One spool Kreinik Gold Balger Cable #002P

¾" sequin pins

Aleene's Tacky Glue

Assorted gold beads, sizes: 4 mm, 6 mm, 8 mm

Tracing paper

Pencil

Serrated knife waxed with candle stub or paraffin

Fine-tip permanent black marker

Ruler

Scissors

Pointed nail file

Toothpicks

Rotary cutter and mat (optional)

Note: Materials listed will make one set of small, medium, and large trees.

1. Trace patterns onto tracing paper and cut out. Place patterns on plastic foam and trace around pattern edges. Cut out trees using serrated knife.

2. Cut 1"-wide strips across width of each solid green fabric. Cut strips into 1" squares and stack according to color.

3. Working from bottom to top of each tree, use the permanent marker to draw horizontal lines across tree, spacing ¼" apart. For each tree, begin at top and use toothpick to apply a thin line of glue over marker line. Center one fabric square over glue line and use nail file to poke fabric ¼" into foam. Continue poking fabric squares until tree front is covered, poking five to six squares per inch and varying fabric colors. Angle file toward tree center when poking squares near edges.

4. To cover back of each tree, place tree on print fabric and trace around edges. Cut out, adding ½" seam allowances. Center and pin fabric to back of tree. Wrap seam allowances over tree edges and glue in place.

5. Glue grosgrain ribbon around tree edges, overlapping ends ¼" at bottom of one side edge.

6. To trim each tree, glue one gold star button to top. Working off spool, tie and glue gold cable end to star button. Thread one 4-mm gold bead on pin, dip pin point in glue and insert partially into tree near edge. Wrap cable around pin several times, add dot of glue, and then press pin in completely. Repeat, alternating sides to zigzag cable to bottom of tree. To add ornaments, thread remaining gold beads onto pins, dip pin points in glue, and press randomly into tree.

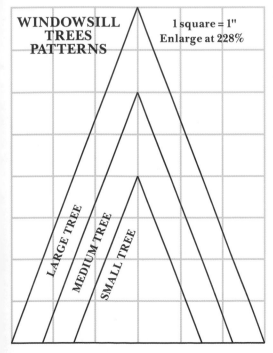

WINDOWSILL TREES PATTERNS

1 square = 1"
Enlarge at 228%

LARGE TREE

MEDIUM TREE

SMALL TREE

Angelic Trio

Materials:
FIMO® oven-bake modeling compound,
  colors: 8 oz. pearl white; 2 oz. mint
  green; 1 oz. flesh; ⅓oz. **each** of
  violet, golden yellow, blue
Mix Quick kneading medium
FIMO® metallic gold powder
Acrylic paint, colors: brown, black, white
Paintbrushes, sizes: soft round, 1 liner
Punch cutters: ¼" circle, ½" star, ⅜" star
8" square lightweight cotton fabric
18" length medium gauge wire (cut into 6"
  lengths)
Oven
Pink chalk
Super glue
Aluminum foil
Round toothpicks
Small piece of cardboard
Insulated baking sheet
Rolling pin
Craft knife
Plastic drinking straw
Scissors
Tracing paper
Wire cutters   Pencil

Note: Materials listed will make three angels. Read instructions before beginning. Prepare clay and roll into sheets before beginning to construct angels. Refer to photo for robe, collar, and decorative accent colors.

1. To prepare violet, yellow, and blue clay colors, mix ⅓ oz. of each color clay with ⅓ oz. pearl white clay and ⅓ oz. kneading medium. For remaining colors, mix five parts clay with one part kneading medium. To mix colors, warm clay in hands for several minutes, and then cut into small pieces. Knead and twist clay until it is a solid color and the texture of soft putty. For each color, roll a handful of softened clay into a ball, and then flatten between hands into a thin pancake. Press one side of pancake on a smooth, slick surface and use rolling pin to roll in one direction three or four times. If clay sticks to surface or rolling pin, rub surface briskly with a dry cloth until clean, pat down any rough clay edges, and roll again. Roll clay 1/16" thick for book, clothes, and hair, and ⅛" thick for wings and base.

2. For **each** angel, crumple one 16" sheet of aluminum foil into a solid cone shape, embedding a toothpick in center for stability. Cone should measure 3½" tall, ⅝" wide at the bottom, and ½" wide at the top; press bottom firmly on table to flatten and add stability. Wrap one end of wire around top of cone twice, folding small pieces of foil over wire to secure. Bend opposite wire end to stick straight up from top of cone.

3. Preheat oven to 250°. Make eyes, book, halos, and horn first; bake while constructing angels. For eyes, roll six balls from pearl clay, each slightly less than 1/16" in diameter and place on baking sheet. For book, cut one 1¼" x 1¾" rectangle from pearl. Place center of rectangle over a piece of folded cardboard to bake book in an open position. For halos, roll three 1/16" x 5" ropes from pearl. Fold each rope in half, twist, and join ends to form circle. For horn, roll one ⅛" x 1¼" rope from pearl and insert toothpick in one end for handling. Press wood end of small paintbrush into opposite end of rope to indent. Holding horn by toothpick and halos and book carefully by edges, coat each piece with gold powder and place on baking sheet with eyes. Bake for 20 minutes. Let cool. Cut toothpick off horn after baking.

4. Trace patterns onto tracing paper and cut out. For **each** angel, cut one 2¼"-base circle from pearl clay. Cover bottom of foil cone with base circle, folding clay up around sides to secure. Press firmly on one 4"-square sheet of foil. Place underskirt pattern on sheet of pearl and cut out using craft knife. Smooth bottom cut edges with fingers. Bring short ends together to form a tube and place over cone, gathering tightly to cone at top and pulling to stretch into soft folds at bottom of cone. Refer to photo for robe, collar, and decoration colors. Place robe pattern on sheet of clay, referring to photo for color, and cut out using craft knife. Press robe on fabric square for texture, and place textured-side up on work surface. Use punch cutters to cut out shapes from contrasting clay colors and decorate robe as desired. Press robe again gently with fabric to texture decorative accents. Shape robe into a cone, overlapping straight edges, and place over underskirt on foil cone. Shape bottom of robe into soft folds.

5. For arms, shape two ¼" x 1¼" rolls from flesh clay. Round one end of each roll for hands. For sleeves, shape two ⅜" x 1¼" rolls from clay in color to match robe. Use paintbrush end to hollow the center of each rope halfway up the length. With paintbrush end in sleeve, gently bend at elbow to form sharp curve. Press arms into sleeves and press tops of sleeves to top back of robe. Cut one 2⅛" circle from clay for collar, referring to photo for color, and follow robe instructions to add texture and decorate. For a decorative collar edge, roll two long thin ropes with colors of choice; twist together and press onto collar edge. Make a small, slightly off-center hole in collar and slip over wire at top of body. With longer side in back, press collar to top of robe. For neck, roll one ⅜" x ⅜" rope from flesh clay and insert toothpick through center. Remove toothpick and slide neck over wire at top of body. Roll a thin rope of mint green clay and wrap around bottom of neck to conceal edge.

6. Cut wings from sheet of pearl clay, smooth edges, and press both sides on fabric to add texture. Use a plastic drinking straw with a small piece cut out of end to make curved indentations in wings, and use the paintbrush handle to make indentations along edges. Press wings to angel's back, holding front of angel with finger under collar while pressing.

7. For **each** head, roll flesh clay into a ⅝" ball, and then form into an egg shape with small end up. Hollow out singing mouth and mouth for horn with a toothpick, and use drinking straw with cut end to make smiling mouth. Press baked eyes into face and press on 1/16" or smaller ball from flesh for nose. Pierce center of head from top to bottom with a toothpick, slide over wire, and press on top of neck. Rub pink chalk on piece of paper to make a small pile of chalk dust. Use soft paintbrush to apply pink chalk dust lightly to cheeks. Form wire at top into loop for hanging, or cut off close to head for standing angels. For hair, cut one 1¼" x 4" strip from sheet of yellow clay. Cut lengthwise into ⅛"-wide strips, and then cut each strip into fringes. Curl fringes by twisting or leave straight and press onto head, arranging and trimming ends as desired. Glue halo on head using a small amount of super glue.

8. Refer to photo and position book in singing angel's arms, press hands together on praying angel, and position horn and hands on angel with horn. Place angels on baking sheet and bake at 250° for 45 minutes to 1 hour. (**Note:** Check pieces often, as under-baking will result in very fragile angels.) Let cool.

9. Using acrylic paints and liner brush, paint eyes with brown circle; add dot of black for pupil. Let dry and add tiny white highlight to each eye. Add tiny freckles with brown, if desired.

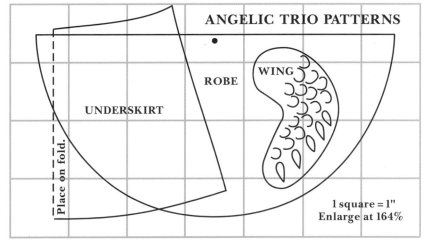

ANGELIC TRIO PATTERNS

UNDERSKIRT

Place on fold.

ROBE

WING

1 square = 1"
Enlarge at 164%

Party Favor Baskets

Materials:

½" x 12" x 36" sheet Styrofoam® brand plastic foam

½ yd. 2⅝"-wide cotton holiday ribbon (for **each** basket)

6" x 11" solid color fabric scrap to coordinate with ribbon (for **each** basket)

12" lengths of assorted ribbons, laces and trims to coordinate with holiday ribbon

Trims of choice: satin ribbon roses, tiny gold pinecones, small ribbon bows

Poster board

Two 12" chenille stems

Serrated knife waxed with candle stub or paraffin

Fine-tip permanent marker

Thread to match handle cover fabric

Ruler

Scissors

Awl

Toothpicks

Low-temp glue gun

Thick craft glue

Sewing machine

Note: Materials listed will make one basket except for plastic foam sheet, which will make 16 baskets.

1. For **each** basket, use fine-tip marker and ruler to mark cutting lines for pieces on plastic foam sheet. Mark one 1½" x 2½" piece for bottom, two 1¾" x 1½" pieces for ends, and two 1¾" x 3½" pieces for sides. Cut out pieces using waxed serrated knife and a sawing motion. Gently sand rough edges with a scrap piece of plastic foam.

2. From poster board, cut one 2¼" x 3¼" piece for basket bottom and one 1⅜" x 2⅜" piece for lining bottom. From fabric, cut one 1¾" x 8" piece for basket lining, one 1⅞" x 2⅞" piece to cover poster board lining bottom, and one 1¾" x 11" piece to cover basket handle. From holiday ribbon, cut one 12" length for outside of basket and one 3¾" length to cover poster board for basket bottom.

3. To construct basket, use glue gun to glue end pieces, and then sides to cut edges of bottom piece.

4. Using craft glue, glue 12" ribbon length to one end of basket and wrap around sides with ¾" of ribbon extending above top basket edge and ⅛" extending below bottom edge. Turn under ribbon end to align with corner and glue in place. Glue ribbon edges to top inside and bottom basket edges, mitering corners and clipping ribbon as necessary. Glue 3¾" ribbon length over poster board basket bottom piece and glue to bottom of basket.

5. To line inside of basket, turn under and glue a ¼" hem along one long edge of lining fabric. Beginning and ending at one corner, glue lining in basket with hemmed edge at top. Place poster board lining bottom piece inside basket to check fit; trim if necessary. Remove from basket, glue fabric over poster board to cover, and glue inside basket.

6. Twist chenille stems together and cut to 6½" length for handle. Fold handle fabric in half lengthwise with right sides facing. Sew together using a ¼" seam allowance. Trim seam allowance, turn, and slide over chenille stem handle. Turn under raw fabric edges and slide fabric up to expose ¾" of chenille stem handle on each end. Use awl to make a ¾"-deep hole in center top edge of each basket side. Glue chenille stem handle ends into holes.

7. Referring to photograph, glue trims and assorted ribbons to basket as desired.

Yo-Yo Mini-Totes

Materials:

¼ yd. 38"-wide unbleached cotton duck fabric (for **each** bag)

Eleven 1½" circles of Christmas print fabric (for tree bag yo-yos)

Twelve 1½" circles of Christmas print fabric (for wreath bag yo-yos)

Eleven 2.5-mm gold beads (for tree bag)

Twelve 2.5-mm red beads (for wreath bag)

8" length ⅜"-wide red satin ribbon (for **each** bag)

⅜" gold star button with shank removed (for tree bag)

Fine-tip permanent red fabric marker

Threads to match fabrics

Sewing machine

Tape measure

Scissors

Straight pins

Hand-sewing needle

Thick craft glue

Iron

1. For **each** tote bag, from cotton duck fabric cut one 8½" x 16" rectangle for bag and one 2" x 11" strip for handle.

2. Finish the two long edges of the bag rectangle with a narrow satin stitch. Turn short ends of rectangle under ¼" twice and hem. Fold rectangle in half with right sides facing and hemmed edges together at top. Sew side seams using a ½" seam allowance. Press bottom fold and press seams open.

3. To make box corners in bottom edge, measure 1¾" from bottom of side seam and stitch across corner as indicated in Illustration. Repeat for remaining corner. Turn and press.

4. Fold handle in half lengthwise with right sides facing. Sew long edges together using a ¼" seam allowance; turn. Press short edges under ¼". Pin handle ends to inside center front and back of tote with ½" of handle extending below top edge. Sew handles in place.

5. Follow instructions on page **25** to make fabric circles into yo-yos. Referring to photo, position yo-yos on bag to form tree or wreath. Remove one yo-yo at a time and glue in place. Let glue dry. Glue one bead to center of each yo-yo.

6. Tie ribbon into a bow and glue to bag as shown in photo.

7. To finish, write "Merry Christmas" in center of wreath using permanent marker, or glue star to top of tree.

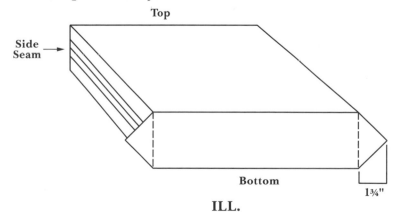

ILL.

Quick & Easy Accessories

If you need just the right favor to fill the stocking of the person who "has everything," take a look at this collection.

For the man on your Christmas list, why not try an eyeglasses case made using quilting techniques? For the ladies, choose from a variety of accessories, including totes to fit inside a purse and business-card holders made from silk ties. Ethnic Bracelets will be much worn and enjoyed by the younger set, and an appliquéd purse or appealing Apple Coin Purse will add a touch of whimsy to your holiday giving.

In addition to finding the perfect presents for those difficult-to-shop-for people, you'll have the added bonus of enjoying your handiwork while you create easy-to-make gifts.

Purse Organizers

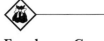

Eyeglasses Case

Materials:
4½" x 26" piece floral print polished cotton
4½" x 13" piece medium-weight polyester batting
Threads to match fabrics
Sewing machine
Ruler   Scissors
Iron   Straight pins

1. With fabric wrong-side-up, center batting crosswise and pin to secure. Fold in half crosswise with right sides facing. Sew long edges together using a ⅜" seam allowance. Press to crease center bottom of bag.
2. To make box corners in bottom edge, position case with bottom crease aligned with side seams as shown in Illustration 1. Pin bottom crease and side seams ½" from point of triangle on each side. Flatten bottom and sew across triangle base. Trim each corner to ¼". Turn and press.
3. Turn open ends under ¼" and topstitch together. Tuck topstitched edge in case to bottom seam to form lining. Press edges.

Purse Tissue Holder

Materials:
6" x 16" piece floral print polished cotton
6" x 16" piece iron-on interfacing
Threads to match fabrics
Scissors
Sewing machine
Iron   Ruler
Straight pins Fabric marker

1. Fuse interfacing to wrong side of fabric. With interfaced side up, mark fold lines with fabric marker as shown in Illustration 2. Referring to Illustrations 2 and 3, fold fabric to the right along line A, and then fold back to left with fold positioned at dashed line B and pin to secure. Fold opposite end of fabric left at line C, back to right at B, and pin to secure. (**Note:** Adjust if necessary to make two pockets the same size.)
2. Referring to Illustration 3, fold fabric extension on right side to the left at dashed line D, covering two pockets and forming one large top pocket. Press folds lightly. Sew layers together across top and bottom edges using a ⅜" seam allowance. Turn large top pocket, carefully pushing out corners. Turn two smaller pockets, pushing out corners. Press tissue cover.

Cosmetic Bag

Materials:
10" x 24" piece floral print polished cotton
10" x 24" piece iron-on interfacing
7" length ¾"-wide Velcro®
Threads to match fabrics
Ruler
Scissors
Sewing machine
Iron
Straight pins

1. Fuse interfacing to wrong side of fabric. Fold fabric in half crosswise with right sides facing. Sew long edges together using a ⅜" seam allowance. Press to crease center bottom of bag.
2. To make box corners in bottom edge, position case with bottom crease aligned with side seams as shown in Illustration 1. Pin bottom crease and side seams 1" from point of triangle on each side. Flatten bottom and sew across triangle base. Trim each corner to ¼". Turn and press.
3. Turn open ends under ¼" and topstitch together. Tuck topstitched edge in bag to bottom seam to form lining. Press edges.
4. Center and pin Velcro® strips inside top edge of purse, close to edge. Topstitch in place around each strip.

Jewelry Case

Materials:
8" x 22" piece floral print polished cotton
7" x 8" piece medium-weight polyester batting
2" length ¾"-wide Velcro®
Disappearing-ink fabric-marking pen
Threads to match fabrics
Sewing machine
Straight pins
Ruler
Scissors   Iron

1. With fabric wrong-side-up, mark line A as shown in Illustration 4. Place fabric right-side-up and lightly mark lines B and C with fabric marker. Sew Velcro® strips along lines B and C, as indicated in Illustration 4.
2. With fabric wrong-side-up, pin batting centered over line A with 8" edges at top and bottom. With right-side-up, fold left end of fabric and batting to right along line A, and then fold back to left, aligning raw fabric edge with line A fold. Fold right end over to left edge, aligning raw edges, and forming large pocket. Press. Sew layers together across top and bottom edges. Trim seams and corners.
3. Turn large pocket and carefully push out corners. Move inside pocket out of way and fold raw edges on either side of pocket under ⅛". Align seams and sew layers together close to edge. (**Note:** You will not be able to sew all the way to each seam.) Turn pocket inside out and push out corners. Press case. Sew down center of pocket from top to bottom.

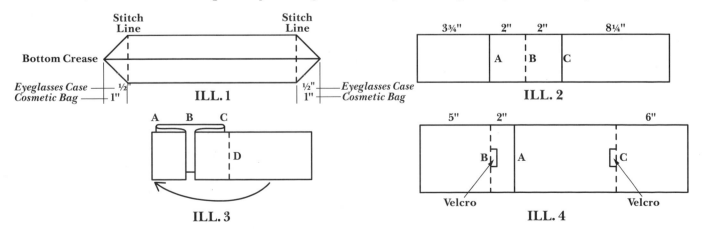

ILL. 1

ILL. 2

ILL. 3

ILL. 4

Purse, Belt, & Earrings

Fabric-Covered Belt & Earrings

Materials:

⅛ yd. **each** 44/45"-wide rayon rose, purple, violet, turquoise, dark green, and coordinating print rayon faux-suede fabrics

¼ yd. 44/45"-wide black faux-suede fabric

1½ yds. antique gold rope trim (cut into three ⅓-yd. lengths)

Two 1¼" antique gold buttons

1 yd. 1¾"-wide black belting

6" length 1"-wide black Velcro®

4 yds. clothesline cord (cut into 15" lengths)

Two 1"-diameter wooden disks painted black (for earrings)

Earring backs

Hot glue gun

Tape measure

Scissors

Iron

Sewing machine

Threads to match fabrics

Belt

1. Cut one 3" x 45" strip from **each** fabric color, including black faux-suede fabric. Fold each strip in half lengthwise with right sides facing and sew long edges together using a ⅝" seam allowance. Turn and cut each tube into 15" and 30" lengths. Slide each fabric tube over one 15" cording length, gathering long tubes to fit.

2. Referring to Illustration, align four gathered and four straight fabric-covered cords in groups, placing seams in back. Sew tubes together tightly across tops, stitching 1½" from edges. Braid the three tube groups together and sew bottom ends tightly to secure. Using two lengths of gold trim, weave into the cords of two braid groups, sewing trim ends to braid ends. Measure braid length and subtract a 1½" seam allowance for each end to determine design area measurement.

3. To determine belt length, measure waist and add 7" to measurement. Subtract design area measurement from belt length measurement to determine length of belting. Cut belting, and then cut in half for each side of belt. Glue each belting length over an end of the braided tubes, overlapping 1½".

4. To cover belting, cut two pieces of black fabric, each 5" wide and 2½" longer than belting. Fold each fabric piece in half lengthwise with right sides facing and use a ⅝" seam allowance to sew long edges together. Trim seam and press with seam in center back. Sew a ⅝" seam across one short end and trim. Turn and slide each piece over belting. Turn under raw fabric edges at ends of braids and use a slipstitch to gather by hand. Pull thread, fitting fabric tightly around belting, and tack in place.

5. To make keep (a belt loop sewn underneath the left side of belt to hold ends in place), cut one 1½" x 4½" piece of black fabric. Fold in half lengthwise and sew long edges together using a ⅜" seam allowance. Turn and tuck raw edges under on both ends. Sew ends to inside of belt at left end. Sew loop side of Velcro® strip inside the left end of the belt, ½" in from the end. Cut one 3" length from hook side of Velcro® strip and sew to outside of right end of belt, ½" from end.

6. Sew buttons to front of belt.

ILL.

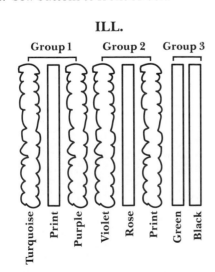

Group 1 — Turquoise, Print
Group 2 — Purple, Violet, Rose
Group 3 — Print, Green, Black

Earrings

1. For each earring, tie one print and three solid tubes (left over from belt) together in an overhand knot. Cut knot from tubes, leaving ends long enough to turn under.

2. Apply hot glue over entire top of one black wooden disk and press knot into glue. Wrap leftover gold trim around knot, hiding ends under knot. Repeat for other earring.

3. Glue fabric-covered discs to backs of earrings.

Easy Appliqué Purse

Materials:

⅓ yd. 44/45"-wide purple moiré taffeta (for purse)
⅓ yd. 44/45"-wide teal moiré taffeta (for lining and appliqué)
6" square black moiré taffeta (for appliqué)
Duncan Scribbles® 3-Dimensional Fabric Writers paint, color: glittering gold
Pellon® Wonder-Under® Transfer Fusing Web
Straight pins
1¼ yds. ¼"-wide gold metallic twisted cording
¾" gold button with shank
Sewing machine
Threads to match fabrics
6" length black elastic cording
Tracing paper
Pencil
Ruler   Iron
Scissors   Measuring tape

Note: Use a ½" seam allowance and sew all seams with right sides facing unless otherwise indicated.

1. To make purse pattern, draw one 7½" x 9" rectangle on tracing paper. Fold rectangle in half lengthwise and cut bottom corners to round. Open pattern and cut two purse pieces **each** from purple and teal taffeta fabrics. Trace heart appliqué patterns onto tracing paper and then trace patterns onto paper backing of iron-on adhesive, tracing a separate pattern for each size of heart. Follow manufacturer's instructions and fuse to fabrics as indicated on patterns. Cut out pieces and remove paper backing.

2. Center extra large teal heart on right side of one purple purse piece and fuse in place. Center and fuse black heart on teal heart, purple heart on black heart, and small teal heart on purple heart.

3. Sew purse front and back pieces together along side and bottom edges. Turn and press top edge under 1". Sew lining pieces together along side and bottom edges; do not turn. Press 1" along top edge toward wrong side. Insert lining in purse, aligning side seams. Pin twisted cording ends between purse and lining at side seams. Fold elastic cording in half to make a loop and pin ends to center of back top edge between purse and lining. Sew top edges of purse and lining together, stitching ¼" from edge. Sew button to purse front in a position to hold elastic loop securely in place.

4. Squeezing paint directly from bottle, outline each heart and add dots as shown in photo.

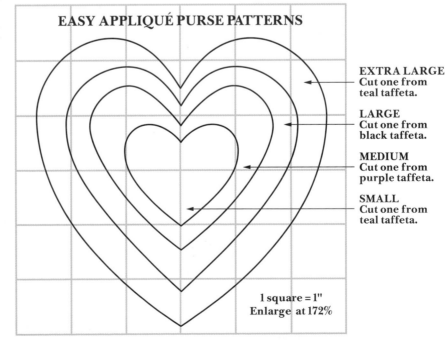

EASY APPLIQUÉ PURSE PATTERNS

EXTRA LARGE
Cut one from teal taffeta.

LARGE
Cut one from black taffeta.

MEDIUM
Cut one from purple taffeta.

SMALL
Cut one from teal taffeta.

1 square = 1"
Enlarge at 172%

Cherry Pincushion & Pin

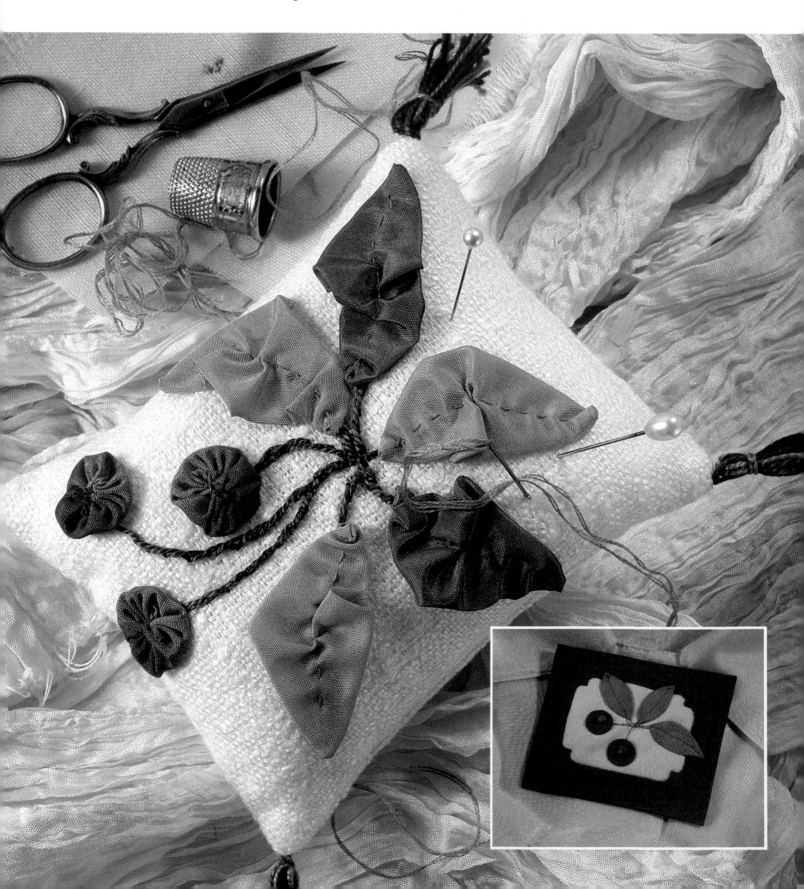

Cherry Pincushion

Materials:

Two 4½" x 5½" pieces off-white fabric (for cushion)
5" length 1½"-wide dark green satin ribbon (cut into 2½" lengths)
7½" length 1½"-wide light green satin ribbon (cut into 2½" lengths)
7" length 2"-wide shaded red satin ribbon
Pearl cotton #5, colors: green to match ribbon, red variegated
Small amount polyester fiberfill
Threads to match fabric and ribbons
Scissors
Straight pins
Sewing machine
Hand-sewing needle
4" square piece of cardboard (for tassel)

1   For cherries, cut three 2" circles from red ribbon. Follow the instructions given on page **25** to make ribbon circles into yo-yos.
2. For leaves, fold each green ribbon length in half lengthwise and sew ends with matching threads as shown in Illustrations 1a and 1b. Trim seam allowance to ⅛" and turn. Using green thread and running stitch, hand-sew one vein in each leaf, gathering slightly to flute leaves.
3. Referring to Illustration 2, pin cherries and leaves to right side of one off-white cushion piece. Hand-sew in place, sewing cherries through centers and leaves through veins and leaving edges loose. Use green pearl cotton to work stem stitch for cherry stems.
4. Sew cushion pieces together with right sides facing, using a ¼" seam allowance and leaving a 2" opening to turn. Clip corners and turn. Stuff lightly and slipstitch opening closed.
5. Make tassels with variegated red pearl cotton, following instructions on page **48**. Sew one tassel to each corner.

ILL. 1a

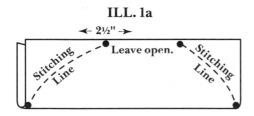

ILL. 1b

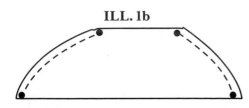

ILL. 2
Top

· · · · · = **Running stitches to gather leaves slightly**
— — — = **Stem stitch**

Cherry Pin

Materials:

Ultrasuede® scraps: 4" x 8" red, 2" square green, 2½" x 3" ivory
Red variegated pearl cotton #5
4" x 8" piece Pellon® Wonder-Under® Transfer Fusing Web
Two 2½" x 2" pieces Pellon® fusible fleece
1¼" bar pin back
Non-stick appliqué pressing sheet or leftover paper backing from transfer web
Red and green sewing threads
Iron
Scissors
Sewing machine
Hand-sewing needle
Pencil

1. Trace patterns onto paper side of transfer web and, following manufacturer's instructions, fuse to wrong side of Ultrasuede® as indicated on patterns. Also trace a 2½" x 2" rectangle for insert and two ⅝" circles for cherries onto transfer web paper. Fuse rectangle to wrong side of ivory Ultrasuede® and circles to wrong side of red Ultrasuede®. Cut out pieces.
2. Center ivory rectangle behind red frame. Place cherries and leaves with right-sides-up on top as shown in Illustration 3. Fuse pieces in place using non-stick pressing sheet.

3. Machine-stitch veins in leaves and stems of cherries with green thread. Use variegated pearl cotton to work one French knot in the center of each cherry.
4. Layer backing (wrong-side-up), both layers of fleece, and appliquéd front (right-side-up). Fuse layers together (center should puff). Machine-stitch around outer edge of pin ¼" from edge.
5. Sew pin back to center back.

ILL. 3

CHERRY PIN PATTERNS (FULL SIZE)

Cut one from red UltraSuede® with center cut out.
Cut 3 leaves from green UltraSuede®
Cut one complete piece for backing.

Ethnic Bracelets & Neclace

Ethnic Bracelets

Abbreviations

beg—begin(ning) **ch**—chain(s)
est—established **pat**—pattern
rep—repeat **rnd(s)**—round(s)
sc—single crochet
sl st—slip stitch
yo—yarn over

Materials:

DMC Pearl Cotton size #5: 1 ball each
  blue #322, and coral #351 for striped
  bracelet; 1 ball each green #911 and
  purple #552 for diamond bracelet
Size B/1 (2.25 mm) aluminum crochet
  hook or size to obtain gauge
8" length ½" macrame cord for each
  bracelet
Yarn needle

Gauge: 8 sc = 1"
Finished size: 9½" to 9¾" circumference

Note: To change colors, always work yo
of color being worked with next color.
Carry color not in use loosely across back
of work, catching in sc as you work.

Striped Bracelet

With blue, ch 76; sl st in first ch to form a
ring, taking care not to twist ch.
Rnd 1: Ch 1; * sc in 2 ch with blue, sc in
next 2 ch with coral; rep from * around,
ending with sl st to beg ch-1.
Rnds 2–10: Rep rnd 1 working sc in
each sc in est color pat. Fasten off leaving a 12" tail of blue thread.
Finishing: Weave in all ends except 12"
tail. Cut cord the length to fit inside
bracelet and insert cord. With right side
of work facing you, sl st opening shut.
Roll seam to inside of bracelet.

Diamond Bracelet

Note: When working with green, work in
the front loop only, and when working
with purple, work in the back loop only.

With green, ch 78; sl st in first ch to form
a ring, taking care not to twist ch.
Rnd 1: Ch 1, sc in each ch around with
green; sl st to beg ch-1.
Rnd 2: Ch 1; * 5 sc with green, 1 sc with
purple; rep from * around, ending with
sl st to beg ch-1.
Rnd 3: Ch 1; * 1 sc with green, 2 sc with
purple; rep from * around, ending with

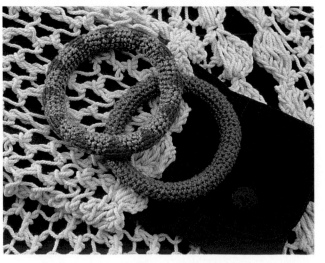

sl st to beg ch-1.

Rnd 4: Ch 1; * 3 sc with green, 3 sc with purple; rep from * around, ending with sl st to beg ch-1.

Rnd 5: Ch 1; * 2 sc with green, 4 sc with purple; rep from * around, ending with sl st to beg ch-1.

Rnd 6: Ch 1; * 1 sc with green, 5 sc with purple; rep from * around, ending with sl st to beg ch-1.

Rnds 7-11: Rep rnds 5-1. Fasten off, leaving a 12" tail of green thread.

Finishing: Work as for striped bracelet.

Necklace for All Seasons

Materials:
3" x 26" piece bias cut osnaburg or muslin (for necklace)
Felt scraps: 3" x 6" dark gold, 3" square medium gold, 4" x 10" dark green, 1½" x 3" light green, 1½" x 3" bright red, 3" x 6" dark red, 2" square medium red, 2" square tan (for charms)
2" square yellow Ultrasuede® (for sun)
Embroidery floss, colors: dark red, bright red, dark green, light green, medium gold, dark gold, bright blue, purple
¼ yd. Pellon® Wonder-Under® Transfer Fusing Web
2" x 4" piece Pellon® fusible fleece
1½ yds. ½" cotton cording
One size 1 snap
Four size 2 snaps
Seven black seed beads (for watermelon)
Fine-tip permanent brown marker
Ivory and black sewing threads
Disappearing-ink fabric-marking pen, tested on Ultrasuede® scrap
Hand-sewing needle
Sewing machine   Iron
Pencil   Scissors

1. Fold cording length in half to find center. (**Note:** Cording is twice the length needed for necklace to allow for turning.) With strip ends of osnaburg at center of cording, fold fabric around cording with right sides facing and matching raw edges. With ivory thread, sew across fabric ends at cording center, and then with zipper foot sew down length of fabric ½" from raw edges. Trim seam allowance on long edge to ⅛". Holding fabric loosely at stitched end, gently pull fabric from covered to uncovered end of cording, turning tube right side out and encasing cording (see Illustration). Cut off uncovered half of cording.

2. Cut ½" of cording off each end and push cording back inside casing. Hand-sew around the casing using running stitch and ivory thread, ¼" in from each end. Tucking raw edges in, pull up running stitches to close ends of tube. Sew size 1 snap half on each end of tube. Sew hole-half of size 2 snap to center front of tube.

3. For charms, trace patterns onto paper side of fusing web and cut out. Fuse to felt or Ultrasuede® as indicated on patterns. Also draw two 2¼" circles for sun on transfer web paper, cut out, and fuse to dark gold felt. Cut out shapes. Refer to photos when finishing each charm.

4. To make sun, use the fabric marker to transfer features to Ultrasuede® face piece. Draw over lines with permanent marker. Layer and fuse one gold circle, rays, fleece circle, and face. Use matching floss to work buttonhole stitches around face and sun rays. Fuse front to remaining gold circle and work buttonhole stitch around outside edges. Sew ball-half of size 2 snap to top back of sun.

5. To make heart, layer and fuse one large heart, medium heart, and small heart. Work buttonhole stitches around all edges with dark red floss. Sandwich fleece between front and remaining large heart piece and fuse together. Work buttonhole stitches with dark red floss around outside edges. Sew ball-half of size 2 snap to top back of heart.

6. To make watermelon, sew black seed beads to red piece with black thread. Layer and fuse one dark green piece, fleece, light green piece, and red piece. Sandwich fleece between front and remaining dark green piece and fuse together. Work buttonhole stitches with matching floss around outside curved edges. Sew ball-half of size 2 snap to back of watermelon.

7. For tree, fuse four tree layers together. Make French knots for ornaments using red, purple, and blue floss colors. Work buttonhole stitches around the outside edge with green floss. Sew ball-half of size 2 snap to top back of tree.

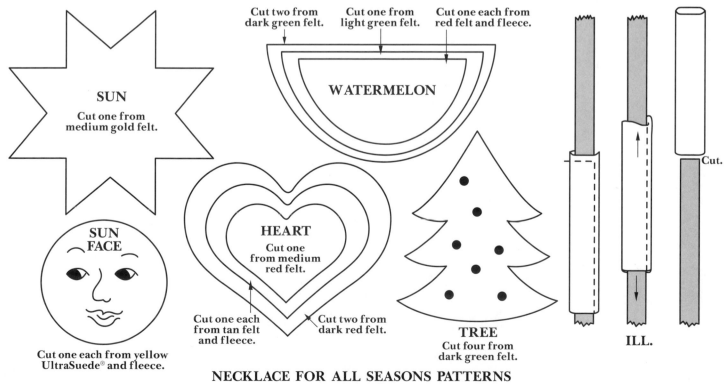

SUN
Cut one from medium gold felt.

SUN FACE
Cut one each from yellow UltraSuede® and fleece.

WATERMELON
Cut two from dark green felt.
Cut one from light green felt.
Cut one each from red felt and fleece.

HEART
Cut one from medium red felt.
Cut one each from tan felt and fleece.
Cut two from dark red felt.

TREE
Cut four from dark green felt.

ILL.
Cut.

NECKLACE FOR ALL SEASONS PATTERNS
(FULL SIZE)

Apple & Watermelon Coin Purses

Apple Coin Purse

Materials:
12" square red nylon fabric (for apple)
Two 5" squares green nylon fabric
  (for leaves)
Two 6" squares low-loft batting
3" length brown leather lacing
1" Velcro® circle
Threads to match fabrics
Fabric glue
Straight pins
Sewing machine
Scissors
Pencil
Tracing paper

1. Trace patterns onto tracing paper and cut out. Cut pieces from fabric and batting as indicated on patterns.
2. To make each apple, with right sides facing and one square batting on top, sew apple pieces together, using a ⅜" seam allowance and leaving an opening for turning. Trim seam, turn, and slipstitch opening closed. Machine satin-stitch around edges of each apple.
3. Sew hook side of Velcro® circle to one leaf, 1" from end. With right sides facing and remaining square batting on top, sew leaf pieces together, leaving an opening for turning. Trim seam, turn, and slipstitch opening closed. Pin bottom half of leaf piece to apple as indicated on pattern. Satin-stitch around edges of leaves, stitching bottom half of leaf to apple to make purse back.
4. Place apple pieces together with sewn leaf on back and edges aligned. Fold top half of leaf over to front and mark placement for loop side of Velcro® closure. Sew Velcro® in place. Satin-stitch edges of apple front and back together along sides and bottom as indicated by Xs on pattern.
5. Apply fabric glue to 1" of leather lacing and insert between leaf and apple on back side of purse.

Watermelon Coin Purse

Materials:
14" square green nylon fabric
  (for watermelon rind)
6" x 12" piece red nylon fabric
  (for watermelon center)
6" square black nylon fabric (for seeds)
⅛ yd. heavy transfer fusing web
7" x 14" piece low-loft batting
1" Velcro® circle
Light green and sewing threads to
  match red and green fabrics
Sewing machine   Pencil
Scissors   Tracing paper

1. Trace watermelon center and rind patterns onto tracing paper and cut out. Cut pieces from fabric and batting as indicated on patterns. Trace 13 seeds onto paper side of fusing web and follow manufacturer's instructions to fuse to wrong side of black nylon fabric. Cut out seeds.
2. Using satin stitch, sew edges of hook side of Velcro® circle to one watermelon center piece as indicated on pattern. Refer to photo and fuse seeds to right side of remaining watermelon center piece, positioning at least 1" from edge. With right sides facing and batting on bottom, sew watermelon center pieces together, using a ⅜" seam allowance and leaving an opening for turning. Trim seam and turn. Slipstitch opening closed.
3. Cut watermelon rind batting piece in half lengthwise. Fold one green nylon rind piece in half lengthwise with right sides facing and place batting on bottom. Sew curved edges together, leaving an opening for turning. Trim seam, turn, and slipstitch opening closed. Repeat for remaining rind piece. Satin-stitch edges of hook side of Velcro® circle to front rind piece 1¼" up from center bottom.
4. With right side of watermelon center piece up, use light green thread to satin stitch side and top edges between Xs to finish. To assemble purse, center unfinished edge of watermelon center piece over back rind piece, aligning Xs with top of rind. Satin-stitch edges in place with light green thread. Satin-stitch curved edges of rind front and back together.

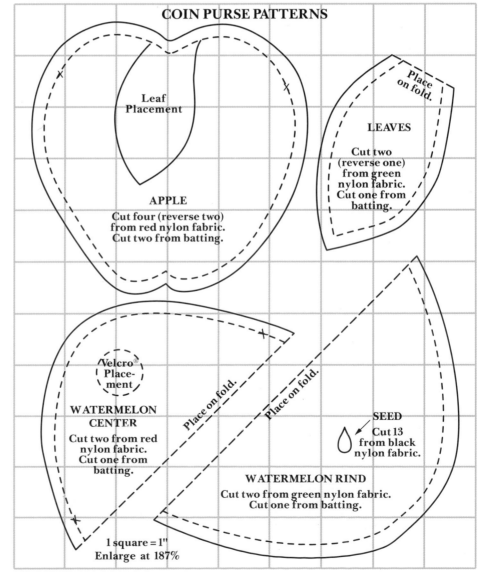

COIN PURSE PATTERNS

Leaf Placement

APPLE
Cut four (reverse two) from red nylon fabric. Cut two from batting.

Place on fold.

LEAVES
Cut two (reverse one) from green nylon fabric. Cut one from batting.

Velcro® Placement

WATERMELON CENTER
Cut two from red nylon fabric. Cut one from batting.

Place on fold.

Place on fold.

SEED
Cut 13 from black nylon fabric.

WATERMELON RIND
Cut two from green nylon fabric. Cut one from batting.

1 square = 1"
Enlarge at 187%

Eyeglasses Cases & Cardholder

Strip-Pieced Case

Materials:
⅞" x 45" strip **each** of tan, turquoise, purple, black, and mauve Ultrasuede® fabrics (for strip piecing)
2" x 3" piece tan Ultrasuede® (for triangle)
6¾" square fusible fleece
6¾" square cotton fabric (for lining)
1 yd. black narrow cording
Threads to match fabrics
9" square muslin   Fabric marker
Sewing machine   Scissors   Iron

1. Enlarge pattern to 7" x 7". Center and trace pattern onto muslin square using fabric marker. Trace top triangle on pattern onto tracing paper and cut out. Cut from tan Ultrasuede®, adding ⅛" seam allowances, and top stitch on muslin as indicated on pattern. Working from triangle down, cut and topstitch Ultrasuede® strips as indicated on pattern, overlapping edges ⅛". After strip piecing is completed, stitch one 7" square to mark outer edge. Trim any strips that extend beyond stitched line.

2. Center fleece on muslin side of pieced strips and follow manufacturer's instructions to fuse in place. With raw edge toward the outside, sew cording along stitched line, beginning and ending at center bottom of square. Fuse lining to fleece. With strip-pieced side up, satin stitch across top edge next to cording.

3. Fold case in half, aligning edges. Satin stitch side and bottom edges closed through all layers, stitching next to cording.

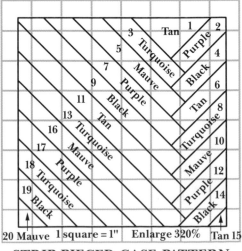

STRIP-PIECED CASE PATTERN

Log Cabin Case

Materials:

1⅛" x 45" strip **each** of turquoise, navy, and burgundy Ultrasuede® fabrics (for log cabin piecing)
6¾" square fusible fleece
6¾" square cotton fabric (for lining)
1 yd. black narrow cording
Threads to match fabrics
9" square muslin
Fabric marker
Sewing machine
Scissors
Iron

1. Enlarge pattern to 7" x 7". Center and trace pattern onto muslin square using the fabric marker. Working from each corner toward center, cut and topstitch Ultrasuede® strips to muslin pattern in log cabin style, overlapping edges ⅛". To begin, cut one 1⅛" square from turquoise strip and topstitch to top right corner of muslin pattern. Cut one 1⅛" square from navy strip and sew in place below turquoise square, overlapping edge. Cut one 1⅛" x 2⅛" piece from burgundy strip and sew along left sides of turquoise and navy squares. Referring to pattern, continue cutting and sewing strips to previous ones to complete each corner. After piecing is completed, stitch one 7" square to mark outer edge. Trim any strips that extend beyond stitched line.

2. Follow steps 2 through 3 for *Strip-Pieced Case* to complete case.

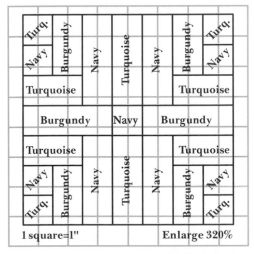

1 square=1"   **Enlarge 320%**

LOG CABIN CASE PATTERN

Silk Tie Business Cardholder

Materials:

Man's silk necktie, at least 3½" wide
½" button with shank in coordinating color
Snap or Velcro® dot fastener
Sewing machine
Threads to match tie
Hand-sewing needle
Scissors   Tape measure   Pencil

1. Place tie face down with wide end of tie at top. See Illustration 1 and measure down 3½" from A to B on each side of tie, marking each point B. Cut straight across tie from B to B, leaving lining in place. Use cutoff tie end for making holder.

2. Fold tie end in half with right sides together and use a ⅝" seam allowance to sew side seam C (see Illustration 2). Finger-press tie flat with seam and point in center and sew bottom seam using a ⅝" seam allowance. Trim seam and turn. Finger-press seam.

3. Fold point down to make flap. Sew button to right side of point for decoration. Sew half of snap to wrong side of point for closure. Sew other half of snap to front of cardholder, aligning with first half of snap.

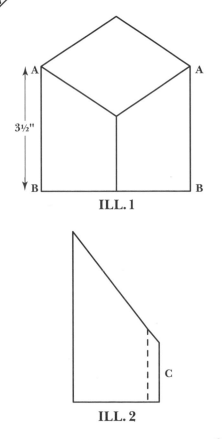

A   A

3½"

B   B

ILL. 1

C

ILL. 2

For Tots to Teens

Come Christmas morning, the children in your life will be convinced that their stockings hold the most wonderful assortment of treasures ever! And you can bask in warm feelings of satisfaction and pride, knowing that gifts you have crafted for them were perfect—both as expressions of your love and as vehicles for your creativity.

If there are wee ones in your household, take a look at the delightful I-Can-Dress-Myself Busy Book. Older children will think you're pretty clever when they see the painted socks and sneakers, which you can match to their wardrobes! For teens, make the Autograph Dog, a sure hit that will bring back memories of your own teen years. Is there a baseball enthusiast in your home? Make the decorative Baseball Card Box to hold his or her collection. It's sure to be a home run! From puppets to pins, from stuffed animals in lacy Victorian costumes to glittering clowns, there is a gift idea for every child.

Victorian
Pig & Bunny Dolls

Victorian Pig Doll

For Ages: 3 yrs. and up

Materials:
½ yd. 44/45"-wide muslin fabric
½ yd. 44/45"-wide chintz fabric
½ yd. 2½"-wide ivory lace
½ yd. ⅛"-wide ivory satin ribbon
14" length ¼"-wide elastic (cut into 3½" lengths)
Two 6-mm black seed beads
Peach acrylic or fabric paint
1"-wide sponge paintbrush
1½" x 2" x 4" wood block
Polyester fiberfill
Threads to match fabrics
Peach and black quilting threads
Hand-sewing needle
Tapestry needle
Sewing machine
Dressmaker's marking pen
Tape measure
Tracing paper
Scissors   Pencil
Straight pins   Iron
Hot glue gun

Note: All seam allowances are ¼" and all seams are sewn with right sides facing unless otherwise indicated.

1. Trace patterns onto tracing paper and cut out. Cut from fabrics as indicated on patterns, transferring pattern markings with dressmaker's pen. Cut one 4½" x 6" piece from chintz for jumpsuit sleeves.
2. Sew sides of ear pieces together, leaving bottom open for turning. Turn and press. For head, sew head pieces together along chin seam. Sew top and back head edges to sides of gusset. Turn under raw edges of nose and nose opening and sew nose in place with a running stitch. Thread hand-sewing needle with peach quilting thread and sew across top of snout from A to B several times, pulling thread to sculpt nose. Repeat to sew from C to D on bottom of snout. Turn under raw edges on ears and slipstitch to top of head. Sew each pair of hand and feet pieces together, leaving straight ends open for turning. Turn and press. Stuff head, hands, and feet firmly with fiberfill.

3. Use sponge brush to paint head, hands, and feet with peach paint. Let dry.
4. Turn under ⅝" on one 6" edge of each sleeve piece and topstitch ½" from fold to make a casing. Insert elastic through casing, pinning ends to raw edges of fabric. Fold each sleeve in half with casing at the bottom and sew side sleeve seam.
5. Repeat sleeve casing instructions to make a casing and insert elastic for bottom of each leg. Sew jumpsuit center front and back seams and inseam. Turn all pieces. Center and pin a sleeve to each side of jumpsuit, aligning top edges. Turn under ⅝" around top edge of jumpsuit to make casing for ribbon. With top edge of lace close to fold and ends in back, topstitch lace to neckline ½" from fold. Thread tapestry needle with ribbon. Insert needle in center front of casing, and thread ribbon through casing and back out center front.
6. Hand-gather bottom edge of head. With 2" x 4" side of block as front, glue head to top of block. Place jumpsuit over block and pull ribbon ends to gather tightly around bottom of head. Tie ribbon into a bow. Glue jumpsuit neckline to head. Glue hands and feet inside cuffs of sleeves and legs.
7. Use black quilting thread to securely sew on one seed bead eye; do not cut thread. Insert needle through head and out opposite eye opening. Pull thread taut to indent eyes and sew on remaining seed bead eye.

Victorian Bunny Doll

For Ages: 3 yrs. and up

Materials:
½yd. 44/45"-wide muslin
½ yd. 44/45"-wide chintz fabric
½ yd. 2½"-wide ivory lace
½ yd. ⅛"-wide ivory satin ribbon
14" length ½" wide elastic (cut into 3½" lengths)
Two 6-mm black seed beads
Tea bags (to dye fabric)
1½" x 2" x 4" wood block
Threads to match fabrics
Natural color and black quilting threads
Polyester fiberfill
Hand-sewing needle
Tapestry needle
Sewing machine
Dressmaker's marking pen
Tape measure
Tracing paper
Scissors   Pencil
Straight pins   Iron
Hot glue gun

Note: All seam allowances are ¼" and all seams are sewn with right sides facing unless otherwise indicated.

1. Trace patterns onto tracing paper and cut out. Cut bunny pieces from muslin and jumpsuit pieces from chintz fabric as indicated on patterns, transferring pattern markings with dressmaker's pen. Cut one 6" square from chintz for jumpsuit sleeves.
2. Sew sides of ear pieces together, leaving bottom open for turning. Turn and press. Fold each ear in half lengthwise and pin to top of one head piece with raw edges even. Sew head pieces to gusset piece. Press and stuff head firmly with fiberfill. Press damp tea bags over head and ears to tea dye. To sculpt nose, thread hand-sewing needle with natural color quilting thread and sew through head from A to B and back across nose to A. Sew through head, going in at A, out at D, in at C, catching thread across nose under needle, out at D, in at C, and out at D, knotting to end. To add whiskers, cut four 12" lengths of natural color quilting thread. Knot two strands together 2½" from one end. Thread long ends onto needle and sew through head at dots. Knot threads together on opposite side, pull thread taut to indent head. Trim ends to 2½". Repeat for second set of whiskers.
3. Sew each pair of hand and feet pieces together, leaving ends open for turning. Turn and press. Stuff hands and feet firmly with fiberfill.
4. Follow steps 4 through 8 of *Victorian Pig Doll* instructions to make jumpsuit and finish.

VICTORIAN PIG & BUNNY DOLLS PATTERNS

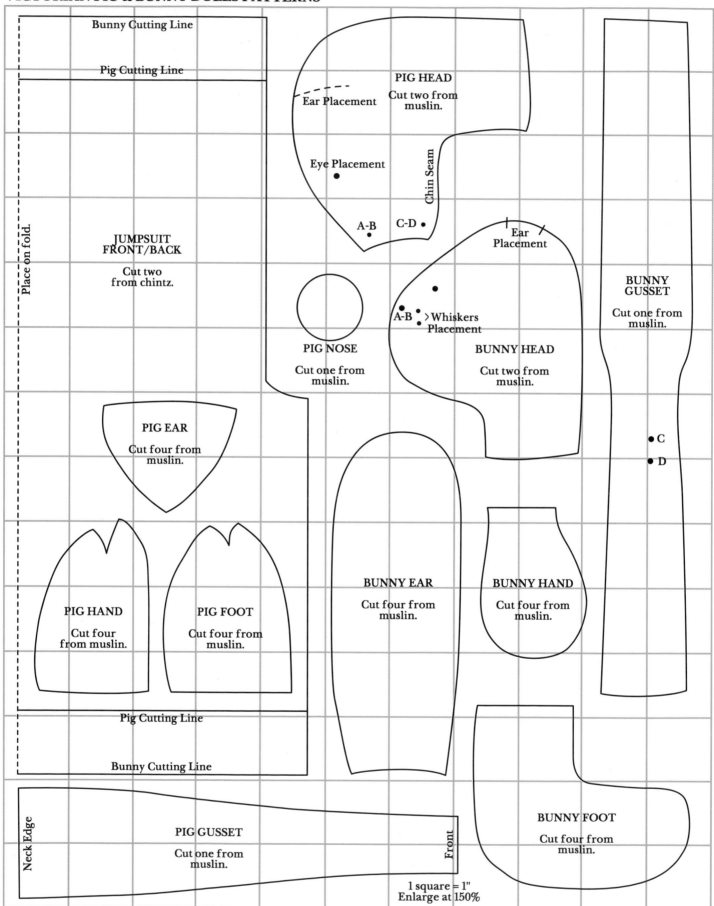

Bunny Cutting Line

Pig Cutting Line

Place on fold.

**JUMPSUIT
FRONT/BACK**

Cut two
from chintz.

PIG HEAD

Cut two from
muslin.

Ear Placement

Eye Placement

Chin Seam

A-B

C-D

Ear
Placement

**BUNNY
GUSSET**

Cut one from
muslin.

A-B

Whiskers
Placement

PIG NOSE

Cut one from
muslin.

BUNNY HEAD

Cut two from
muslin.

C

D

PIG EAR

Cut four from
muslin.

PIG HAND

Cut four
from muslin.

PIG FOOT

Cut four from
muslin.

BUNNY EAR

Cut four from
muslin.

BUNNY HAND

Cut four from
muslin.

Pig Cutting Line

Bunny Cutting Line

Neck Edge

PIG GUSSET

Cut one from
muslin.

Front

BUNNY FOOT

Cut four from
muslin.

1 square = 1"
Enlarge at 150%

Satin Ribbon Clown

For Ages: 3 yrs. and up

Materials:
MPR SatinRibbon™, colors: teal,
 cranberry, purple, navy, old gold
MPR Tissue Twist™, 12"-length white
1¼" wood bead with hole
Strawberry color mini curly hair
Five ⅝" gold jingle bells
Seven ¼" white pom-poms
1 yd. 24-gauge gold wire
4 oz. white rice
Low-temperature glue gun
Scissors
Drawing paper
Pencil
White sewing thread
Hand-sewing needle

1. To make legs, cut one 8"-length each of teal and cranberry ribbons. Glue one short end of teal ribbon to one short end of cranberry ribbon, overlapping 1". Overlap long edges ½" to form a tube and glue. Turn under a 1" hem on one short end and secure tightly with wire ½" from end. Fill tube half full with rice. Turn under a 1" hem on remaining open end and secure with wire ½" from end.
2. To make arms, repeat directions for legs using one 6" length **each** of navy and old gold ribbons.
3. Cut one 16"-length of wire. Gather arms and legs together at centers, evenly distributing rice. Secure centers together with wire, leaving wire ends long. Slide wood bead over wire ends and glue bead to arms. Glue curly hair to top of bead.
4. Trace hat pattern onto drawing paper. Cut one 5" length of purple ribbon and glue to traced pattern. Let glue dry, and then cut out hat pattern. With ribbon on the outside, overlap straight edges ½" and glue. Glue hat to top of head. Cut one 4"-length of gold wire and twist ends together to make a loop. Slide one jingle bell over wire ends and glue to top of hat. Evenly space and glue pom-poms down center front of hat.
5. To make collar, untwist Tissue Twist. Fold in half lengthwise twice. With needle and thread, sew a gathering thread along center of twist through fold. Place around neck, pull thread to gather tightly, and knot thread ends together. Cut along first fold line and fluff layers.

6. Cut four ½" x 1½" strips of purple ribbon. Fold each strip in half lengthwise and glue around tops of arm and leg cuffs to cover wire. Glue a jingle bell inside each cuff.

**SATIN RIBBON
CLOWN PATTERN
(FULL SIZE)**

HAT

105

Baby Dinosaur Puppets

For Ages: 3 yrs. and up

Materials (for **each** puppet):
Three 12" squares red **or** purple Tempo foam-backed nylon fleece fabric or sweatshirt fleece backed with fusible tricot interfacing (for body)
12" square yellow **or** green Tempo foam-backed nylon fleece fabric or sweat-shirt fleece backed with fusible tricot interfacing (for fins and paws)
Two ¼" round buttons (for eyes)
8" length black rickrack (for teeth)
Polyester fiberfill
Threads to match fabric
Carpet or upholstery thread (to sew on eyes)
Air-soluble marker
Sewing machine
Scissors
Pencil
Tracing paper
Tape measure
Iron
Straight pins

Note: All seam allowances are ¼" and all seams are sewn with right sides facing unless otherwise indicated.

1. Trace patterns onto tracing paper and cut out. Cut side/back and front body pieces from red or purple fabric and fins and paws from yellow or green fabric as indicated on patterns. Transfer pattern markings with air-soluble marker.
2. Sew paws to front piece and side/back pieces. Sew rickrack along curved seamline of front piece between dots. Sew fin pieces together, leaving straight edge open. Clip curves, trim seam, turn, and press.
3. For red dinosaur, leave dart on top of head open. Sew center seam from lower edge to dart and from dart to nose. With raw edges even, pin and sew fins across front dart edge between dots. Pin and sew dart closed, matching center seams.
4. For purple dinosaur, sew dart on head for each side/back piece. With raw edges even, pin and sew fins along center seam between dots. Pin and sew side/back piece together from lower edge to nose.
5. Pin front to back, matching paws and dots. Sew, trim points, and turn. Turn under ½" on lower edge and machine hem. Sew along topstitch lines to define head and arms. Stuff head with fiberfill.

6. To finish, refer to pattern and sew on one button eye securely, using one strand carpet or upholstery thread; do not cut. Insert needle through head and out opposite eye opening. Pull thread taut to indent eyes and sew on remaining button eye.

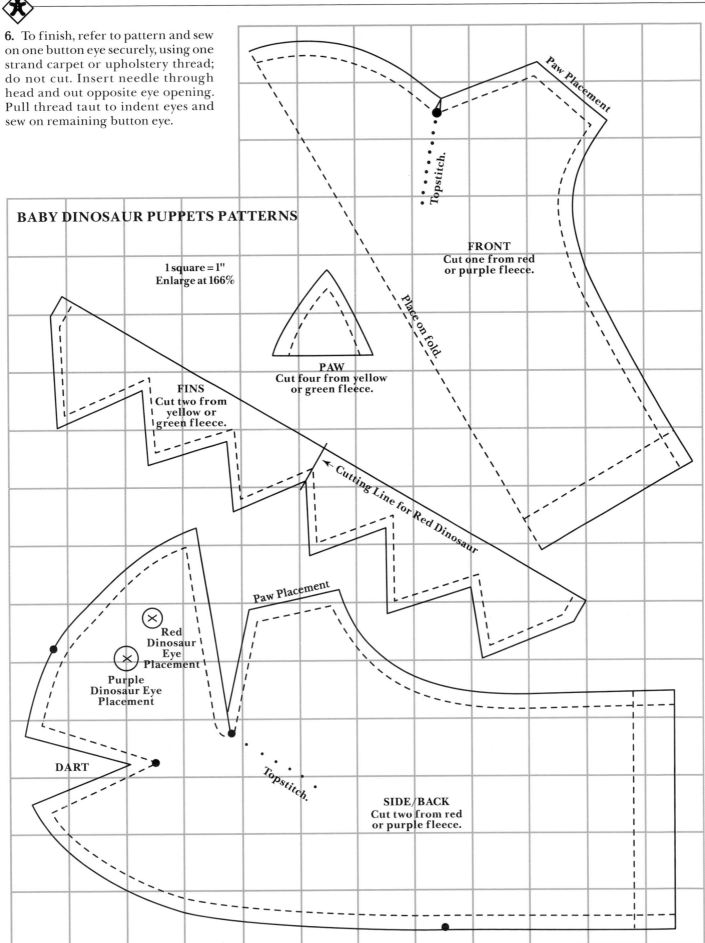

BABY DINOSAUR PUPPETS PATTERNS

1 square = 1"
Enlarge at 166%

FRONT
Cut one from red or purple fleece.

Paw Placement

Place on fold.

Topstitch.

PAW
Cut four from yellow or green fleece.

FINS
Cut two from yellow or green fleece.

Cutting Line for Red Dinosaur

Red Dinosaur Eye Placement

Purple Dinosaur Eye Placement

Paw Placement

DART

Topstitch.

SIDE/BACK
Cut two from red or purple fleece.

107

Smocked Sunglasses Case

Materials:

½ yd. 6"-wide white cotton trim, scalloped on both edges

Pleating machine or smocking transfer dots with rows ⅜" apart

DMC embroidery floss, each color listed in color key

8" x 12" piece white felt

White and contrasting color sewing threads

Hand-sewing needle

Darning needle, size 3 to 9

Sewing machine   Iron

Scissors

1. Mark center of fabric with contrasting thread. Use contrasting thread and even, but not tight, tension to gather 15 rows of pleats for 6" to 6¼" with approximately 126 pleats.

2. To smock design, use two strands of floss for backsmocking and for beach umbrella pole and four strands of floss for remaining smocking. Refer to color key, smocking chart, and stitch illustrations on page **141** to work stitches as indicated in instructions. Each gathering thread corresponds with one numbered row on chart. Leave two pleats on each end of fabric unstitched to allow for seam.

3. With white floss, backsmock (on wrong side of fabric) every row along gathering thread line **except** row 4.

4. Count 21 pleats to right of center mark to begin top of palm tree. Work tree top and trunk with cable stitches, beginning each row with a down stitch. Stack cables close together, fitting five rows of cables between two gathering threads.

5. Work beach horizon line with stem stitch, extending to two pleats from end of fabric.

6. To work each line for waves, begin at horizon line and cable three, trellis three up, cable one, trellis three down; repeat across.

7. Work sun with a stacked cable stitch. For cloud line, cable across from sun to two pleats from end of fabric; cables do not stack.

8. For beach umbrella, begin at arrow to make left yellow panel as follows: cable one, trellis up five, cable one, tie off. Return to starting point, move over one pleat and cable one, trellis up four, and tie off. Return as before, beginning

slightly below previous cable, cable one, trellis up two, and tie off. For center section, use green floss and begin near top of umbrella. Continue first trellis started with yellow, beginning just beneath top yellow cable stitch. Trellis down five, cable one, and tie off. Continue second yellow trellis with green, working down three and cabling one. Fill in with three stitches. Make right yellow panel with two trellis lines and one extra cable stitch. Work umbrella pole with tan and a trellis stitch.

9. Work beach ball with stacked fuchsia cable stitches.

10. Remove gathering threads from smocked design. Fold in half with right sides facing and sew ends together using a ⅛" seam allowance. Turn.

11. To make lining for case, fold felt in half lenthwise. Use a ½" seam allowance to sew long edges together to make a tube. Fold top half of tube right side out over bottom half, aligning ends. Sew ends together, stitching close to edge. Insert lining in smocked piece and tack together at seam line.

Color Code

DMC	Color
◆ 911	green
⊞ 3765	blue
◖ 434	brown, lt.
◩ 740	orange
◉ 742	yellow
◠ 738	tan
◎ 917	fuchsia
★ 602	hot pink

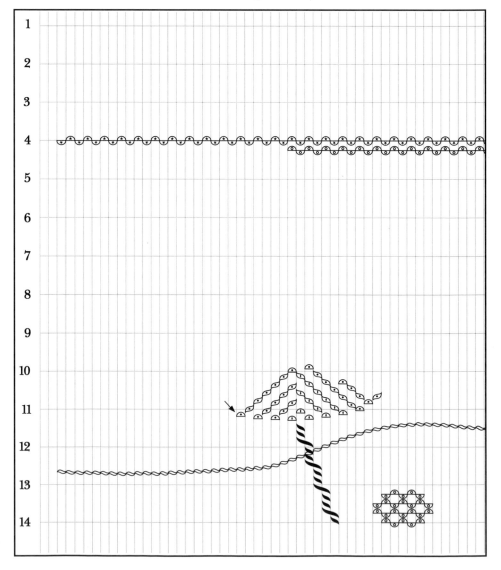

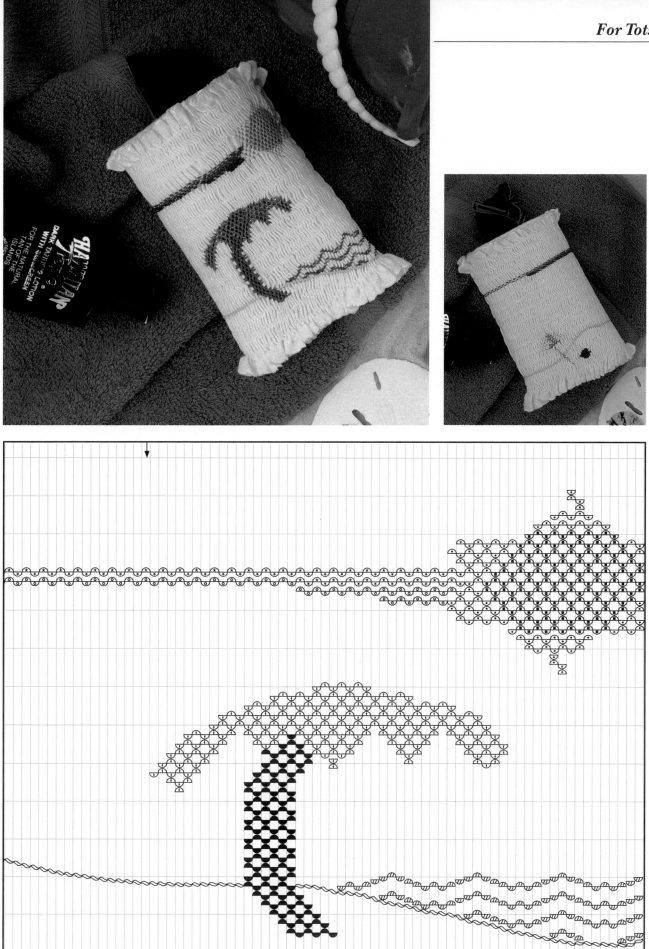

Gifts for Baby

Vinyl Teddy Bear Toy

For ages: 18 mos. to 3 yrs.

	DMC	Color
○	954	green
╲	894	pink
∟	3341	orange
•	745	yellow
X	809	blue
●	317	gray

Fabric: Two 6" x 8" sheets 14-count Vinyl-Weave™ from Crafter's Pride
Stitch Count: 70H x 50W
Design Size: 14-count 5" x 3⅝"

Instructions: With the weave of both vinyl sheets running in the same direction, cross stitch front and back designs using two strands of floss. Work all backstitching, except outline, using two strands 317.

Materials:
Darice "Teddy Bears' Picnic" electronic music button
Polyester fiberfill
Small sharp scissors

1. Complete all stitching following directions given.
2. Align stitched front and back with wrong sides together. Leaving bottom edge open for stuffing, use a double running stitch and two strands 317 to stitch outline through both layers of vinyl. Knot

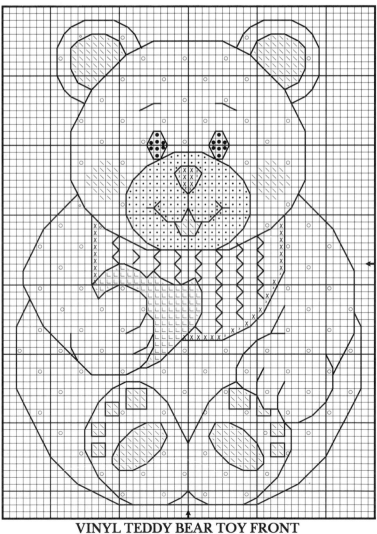

VINYL TEDDY BEAR TOY FRONT

floss and hide knot between layers to begin and end. Trim vinyl one square beyond stitching on sides and top, and four squares beyond bottom of bear.

3. Stuff bear with fiberfill and insert electronic music button, positioning under bib.

4. Stitch bottom opening closed using a double running stitch and two strands 317. Trim vinyl one square beyond stitching.

Carousel Sippee Cup and Bib

DMC		Color
♥	210	violet, lt.
C	776	pink, med.
H	564	jade, vy. lt.
■	518	Wedgwood, lt.
X	726	topaz, lt.
•	white	white
—	3761	sky blue, lt.
I	3078	golden yellow, vy. lt.

Sippee Cup
Fabric: 14-count vinyl insert for sippee cup by Crafter's Pride
Stitch count: 37H x 96W
Design size: 14-count 2⅝" x 6⅞"

Bib
Fabric: 14-count pink baby bib from Crafter's Pride
Stitch count: 102H x 143W
Design size: 14-count 7¼" x 10¼"

Instructions: Cross stitch using two strands of floss. Backstitch using one strand 518.

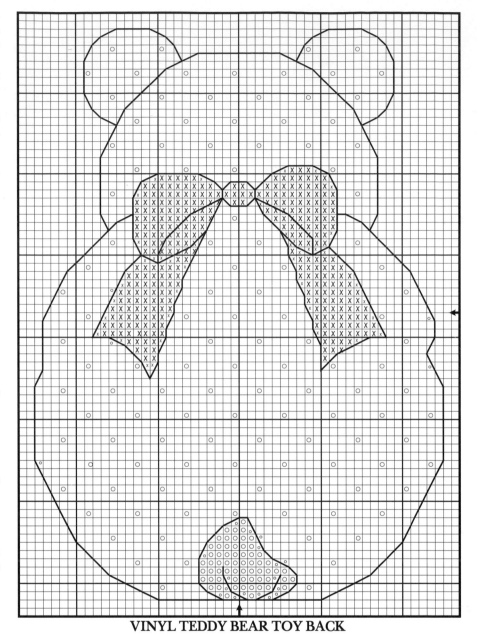

VINYL TEDDY BEAR TOY BACK

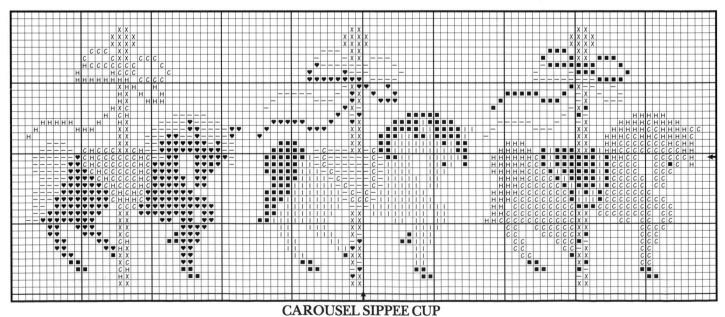

CAROUSEL SIPPEE CUP

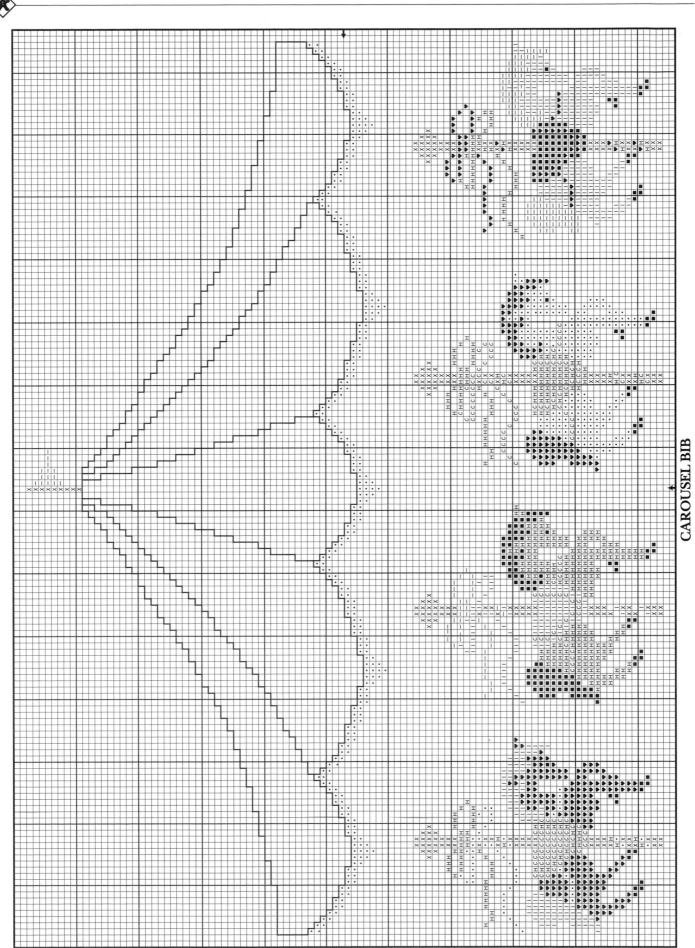

CAROUSEL BIB

Painted Sneakers

Materials:
Duncan Scribbles® 3-Dimensional
    Fabric Writers paint, colors: chiffon
    green, bright blue, black, delicate
    rose, very periwinkle, watermelon,
    shimmering teal, tropical yellow
Size 6 flat fabric paintbrush
High-top white sneakers
Tracing paper
Graphite paper
Pencil

1. Trace alligator pattern onto tracing
paper. Transfer pattern lightly to heel
of right shoe using graphite paper. Reverse pattern and transfer to heel of
left shoe, omitting bow.
2. Paint alligators with two coats of
shimmering teal and bow with two
coats of watermelon, letting dry between coats. Squeezing paint directly
from bottle, outline alligators and bow
with black. Add black dots to shoes
around alligators.
3. Referring to photo, use all paint colors and add dots, waves, and lines along
seams of both shoes. Let dry thoroughly
before wearing.

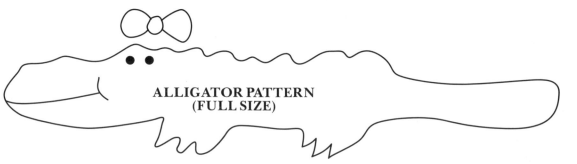

**ALLIGATOR PATTERN
(FULL SIZE)**

Painted Socks

Materials:

Thin cotton anklet socks in colors of
  your choice
Duncan Scribbles® 3-Dimensional Fabric
  Writers paint, colors: white, black,
  neon yellow, neon pink, neon orange,
  gold platinum, Christmas red,
  Christmas green, bright green
Partial roll of bathroom tissue (large
  enough to stretch sock tightly when
  inserted in sock cuff)
Aluminum foil

1. Wash and dry socks; do not use fabric softener. Turn inside out.
2. Cover tissue roll with aluminum foil. Pull cuff of one sock over covered roll, stuffing foot of sock inside roll.
3. Refer to photo to choose pattern and colors for each pair of socks. Squeezing paint directly from bottles, paint a thick line around cuff near edge, and then paint remaining design areas. Let dry completely while stretched over roll. Remove from roll and repeat for each sock.
4. Turn socks and fold down cuffs. To launder, wash in warm water; line dry.

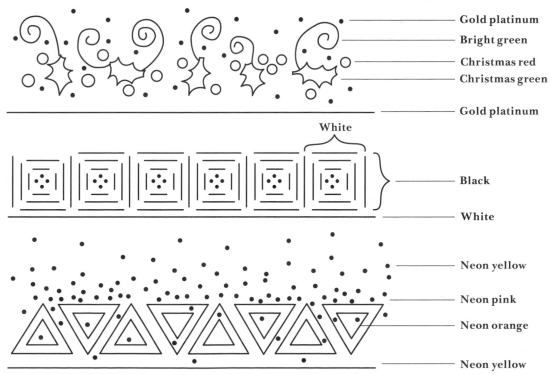

PAINTED SOCKS PATTERNS (FULL SIZE)

Gold platinum
Bright green
Christmas red
Christmas green

Gold platinum

White

Black

White

Neon yellow

Neon pink

Neon orange

Neon yellow

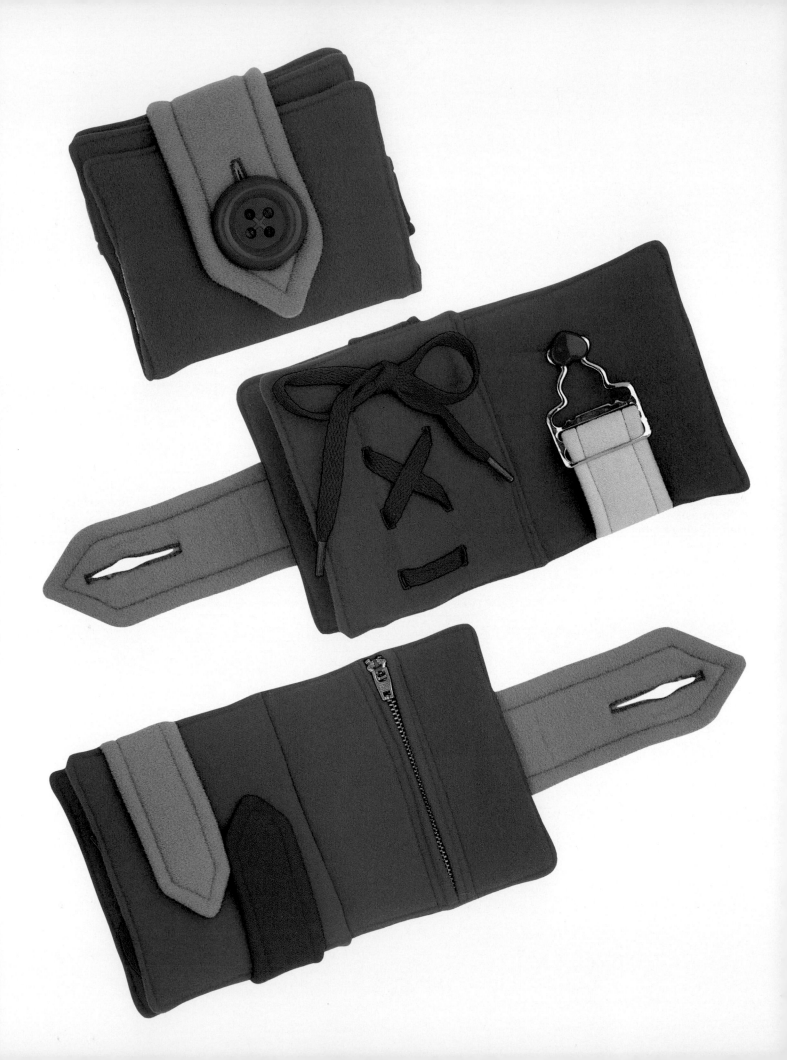

I-Can-Dress-Myself Busy Book

For Ages: 18 mos. to 5 yrs.

Materials:
Two 12" squares blue Tempo foam-backed nylon fleece fabric or sweatshirt fleece backed with fusible tricot interfacing
12" square **each** green, red, and yellow Tempo foam-backed nylon fleece fabric or sweatshirt fleece backed with fusible tricot interfacing
1½"-wide overall hook
⅝" red heart-shaped plastic button
1⅜" red round plastic button
30" long red shoelace
5"-long zipper
Two Velcro® dots
Threads to match fabrics
Carpet or upholstery thread (to sew on buttons)
Hand-sewing needle
Sewing machine
Scissors
Tape measure
Straight pins

Note: All seam allowances are ¼" and all seams are sewn with right sides facing unless otherwise indicated.

1. From blue fabric, cut one 6" x 10" piece for outside cover, two 3" x 6" pieces for zipper page, and three 6" x 5" pieces for remaining pages. From green fabric, cut two 5½" x 3" strips for outside strap and two 4½" x 2" strips for inside strap. Cut one end of each strap piece into a point. From red fabric, cut two 4½" x 2" strips for an inside strap, cutting one end of each piece into a point. From yellow fabric, cut two 5" x 2" strips for overall strap.

2. To make outside strap, sew outside strap pieces together along sides and pointed end, leaving straight end open for turning. Clip point, turn, and press. Topstitch around strap ¼" from edge. Make one 1⅝"-long lengthwise buttonhole with red thread, 1" from point. Center strap on right side of one 6" edge of outside cover piece referring to Assembly Diagram. Sew in place aligning raw edges.

3. To make inside front cover page with overall hook, sew long edges of yellow strap pieces together. Turn and press. Topstitch ¼" from long edges with red thread. Slide overall hook onto strap. Make a loop with strap and pin raw edges to center top of one blue page piece referring to Assembly Diagram. Sew in place ⅛" from edge. Using carpet thread, sew heart button securely to page piece in position corresponding to hook. Knot thread and test button by pulling to make certain it is securely anchored.

4. To make inside back cover page, baste 3" x 6" pieces together along one long edge referring to Assembly Diagram. Follow manufacturer's instructions to insert zipper in center of basted edge. Clip basting threads.

5. Pin inside cover pages to outside cover with center seam allowances turned under. Sew together along outside edges. Trim corners, turn, and press edges.

6. On one remaining blue piece for page 2, mark eight ⅜" buttonholes in center of page as shown in Assembly Diagram. Make buttonholes using red thread. Thread shoe lace through holes and tie into a bow at bottom of page. Sew across top of shoe string to secure. For remaining page, sew each pair of 4" strips together, leaving straight edges open. Clip, turn, and press. Topstitch ¼" from side and pointed end edges. Pin straps to page, aligning raw edges as shown in Assembly Diagram. Sew straight ends to page, ⅛" from edge. Sew hook side of a Velcro dot under point of each strap. Pin shoelace and straps to pages to avoid catching in seam during assembly. To finish center page, sew remaining blue piece to blue piece with shoelace, leaving one side open as shown in Diagram. Clip corners and turn. Topstitch close to sewn edges.

7. To assemble book, insert raw edges of center page into opening in center of book cover with seams facing back cover. Stitch in-the-ditch to secure. Topstitch ¼" from seam on each side to form spine of book. Topstitch close to edges of cover.

8. Close book and mark placement for round button on front cover. Sew button securely in place through top layer of fabric only, using carpet thread. Knot thread and test button to make certain it is securely anchored.

BUSY BOOK ASSEMBLY DIAGRAM

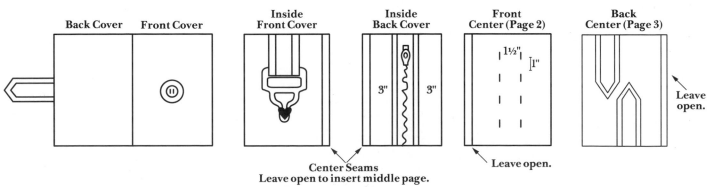

Whimsical Menagerie

Felt Animal Pins

General Materials:
Pin back (one for **each** pin)
Tracing paper
Lightweight cardboard
Soft pencil
Water-soluble fabric marker
Cotton swab
Polyester fiberfill
Scissors
Fabric glue
Toothpicks
Threads to match felt
Hand-sewing needle

General Instructions:
1. Trace pattern pieces on page **119** onto lightweight cardboard and cut out. Number each piece and mark color. Place each piece on appropriate color felt and trace around edges, using pencil for colored pieces and water-soluble marker for white pieces. (**Note:** This will be wrong side of each piece.) Cut out pieces. Use cotton swab dipped in water to dissolve water-soluble marker lines.
2. To assemble each pin, position pieces as on each Layout Illustration and glue or sew as indicated in individual instructions. To glue felt pieces, thin fabric glue with an equal part water. Apply glue with flat edge of toothpick to wrong side of pieces. To sew pieces together, use matching thread. Insert needle through side edges of felt rather than bringing needle through to the top. Refer to each Layout Illustration and embroider facial details as instructed.
3. Sew pin back to center back of each assembled pin to finish.

Dog Pin
Materials:
4" square gray felt
2" x 3" piece white felt
1" square pink felt
6" length ⅛"-wide red satin ribbon
Three ⅛" black half-ball beads
    (for eyes and nose)

1. Glue upper face to under face, sandwiching top edge of tongue between layers. Glue bottom edge of under face to top edge of upper tummy. Glue

assembled pieces to under tummy, and then to front body.
2. Sew edges of layers together as follows: top of cheeks to under face, points of upper tummy to under tummy, and lower edge of under tummy to front body. Backstitch across top of feet.
3. Slipstitch front to back from shoulder to shoulder, leaving top open. Stuff firmly and glue opening closed.
4. Glue eyes and nose in place. Tie ribbon into a bow and tack to chin.

Cat Pin
Materials:
3" x 4" piece white felt
4½" x 3" piece tan felt
½" square pink felt
Black embroidery floss
Blue metallic thread
6" length ⅛"-wide blue satin ribbon
7-mm gold jingle bell

1. On top front piece, glue cheeks in place and pink square to wrong side of mouth opening. Satin-stitch nose with two strands black floss and eyes with metallic blue thread. Glue top front to front.
2. Sew edges of cheeks and tummy to top front. Backstitch between paws and across tops.
3. Glue front and back tails together, and then glue on tail tops.

BEAR PIN PATTERN (FULL SIZE)

Front Cutting Line

Cut two.

Tan

Stitching Line →

CAT PIN PATTERN (FULL SIZE)

4

2

3

CAT LAYOUT ILL.

Front Cutting Line

FRONT/BACK Cut two (reverse one).

Tan

3

DOG PIN PATTERNS (FULL SIZE)

4

5

6

3

2

1

DOG LAYOUT ILL.

FRONT/BACK BODY

Cut two.

1

Gray

UNDER TUMMY

2

White

UPPER TUMMY

3

White

UPPER FACE

5

White

Pink

6

TONGUE

4

UNDER FACE Gray

Top

4 White

TAIL TOP

Cut out.

TOP FRONT

2

White

Stitching Line

Paw   Paw

Top

4 White

TAIL TOP

White

1

CHEEKS

4. Slipstitch front to back around body, leaving top open. Stuff firmly and glue opening closed. Backstitch across base of tail. Tack top of tail to back of head.
5. Wrap ribbon around neck, knotting in front. Glue ribbon ends to tummy. Sew bell to knot of ribbon.

Teddy Bear Pin
Materials:
3½" x 5½" piece tan felt
10" length ½"-wide decorative red ribbon
Two black seed beads
Black embroidery floss
Powder blush makeup

1. Sew seed beads to head for eyes. Satin-stitch nose with two strands black floss and mouth with one strand black floss.
2. Sew edges of front and back together, leaving an opening for stuffing. Stuff firmly and glue opening closed. Back-stitch across tops of legs.
3. Apply blush to cheeks. Beginning and ending below chin, wrap ribbon around bear, crisscrossing in back. Knot ends in front.

119

Autograph Dog

Materials:
¼ yd. 44/45"-wide pink cotton fabric
⅔ yd. ⅝"-wide light blue satin ribbon
Two 9-mm black animal eyes
9-mm black animal nose
Polyester fiberfill
Hand-sewing needle
Pink sewing thread
Sewing machine
Dressmaker's marking pen
Scissors   Pencil
Ink pen with clip   Tracing paper

1. Trace patterns onto tracing paper and cut out. Cut pieces from pink fabric as indicated on patterns. Use dressmaker's pen to transfer pattern markings to body pieces.

2. Sew seams with right sides together, using a ¼" seam allowance. Sew each pair of ear pieces together, leaving open at top. Clip curves, turn, and press. Baste open ends closed. Sew tail pieces together, leaving open at base. Clip curves, turn, and press. Stuff with fiberfill. Baste ears and tail to one body piece with raw edges even. Sew body pieces together, leaving a 3" opening in stomach edge. Clip curves and turn. Follow manufacturer's instructions to attach eyes and nose at markings. Stuff dog firmly with fiberfill and slipstitch opening closed.

3. Wrap ribbon around dog's neck and tie into a bow. Clip pen onto ribbon.

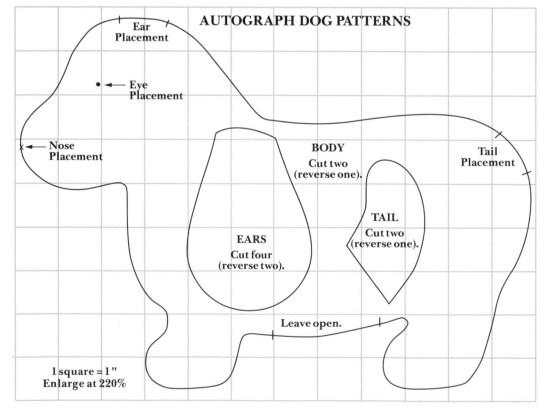

AUTOGRAPH DOG PATTERNS

Ear Placement

Eye Placement

Nose Placement

BODY
Cut two (reverse one).

Tail Placement

TAIL
Cut two (reverse one).

EARS
Cut four (reverse two).

Leave open.

1 square = 1"
Enlarge at 220%

Spot the Dog

For Ages: 3 yrs. and up

Materials:
¼ yd. 44/45"-wide rust color brushed
    fabric
1" square red felt (for tongue)
6" square black felt (for spots and nose)
6" square transfer fusing web
5" circle heavy batting
Two 12-mm wiggle eyes with shank
Polyester fiberfill
Threads to match fabrics
Brown button and carpet thread
Hand-sewing needle with large eye
Sewing machine
Pencil
Iron   Tape measure
Scissors   Compass
Tracing paper   Chalk pencil

Note: All seam allowances are ½" and
all seams are sewn with right sides facing unless otherwise indicated.

1. Trace patterns, except nose and
tongue, onto tracing paper, transferring pattern markings with pencil on
paw, and cut out. Cut pieces from
brushed fabric as indicated on patterns.
From brushed fabric cut two 5" circles
for the head, one 4" circle for the back
end of body and one 4⅜" circle for the
front end of body.

2. Trace nose and tongue patterns onto
paper side of fusing web. Use compass
to draw five circles for spots, ranging in
size from 1" to 1¼", on web paper. Cut
out patterns and follow manufacturer's
instructions to fuse to wrong side of
felt. Cut out pieces. Fuse nose to one
head circle, 1¾" down from top edge.
Fuse tongue to head ¾" below nose.
Randomly fuse three spots to body and
two to one tail piece. Use chalk pencil to
draw line from nose to tongue and
curved edges of mouth. Using black
thread, machine satin-stitch edges of
spots, nose, and mouth and detail lines
on face.

3. Sew tail pieces together, leaving end
open for turning. Clip curves, turn, and
stuff lightly with fiberfill. With raw
edges even, sew tail to center of back
edge of body. Sew bottom seam of body
from each end toward center, leaving a
2" opening in center for turning. Sew
body front and back circles to body

piece. Turn and stuff firmly with fiberfill. Slipstitch opening closed.

4. Sew each pair of ear pieces together,
leaving straight edge open. Trim seams
and turn. Sew a gathering stitch along
bottom of each ear, ¼" from edge, and

pull to gather to 1½". Aligning raw
edges, sew ears close together at top of
head. Layer head front (right-side-
down), batting circle, and back (right-
side-up) and sew around edges. Cut a
slit in center of head back and turn.

121

Hand-sew head front to body. Turn down points of ears and tack in place. Sew wiggle eyes above nose.

5. Sew each pair of paw pieces together, leaving straight edge open. Trim seams and turn. Stuff lightly with fiberfill. Turn under raw edges and slipstitch closed. To make toes on each paw, thread needle with button and carpet thread and knot end. Bring needle through paw from bottom to top at point A, wrap thread over end of foot, and reinsert through foot from bottom to top at point A, pulling thread taut. Insert needle through layers of paw, and repeat for point B. Knot thread end securely. Hand-sew paws to bottom of dog.

SPOT THE DOG PATTERNS
(FULL SIZE)

TONGUE
Cut one from red felt.

EARS
Cut four from rust brushed fabric.

NOSE
Cut one from black felt.

TAIL
Cut two from rust brushed fabric.

Bottom

BODY
Cut one from rust brushed fabric.

Place on fold.

A   B

PAWS
Cut eight from rust brushed fabric.

Back

Rosette Accessories

Materials:

Lightweight white cotton knit fabric:
  2½"-3½" x 18" piece (for **each**
  flower); 3" square (for **each** leaf)
Duncan Scribbles® 3-Dimensional
  Fabric Writers paint, colors: bright
  yellow, bright orange, light pink,
  lipstick pink, purple, light
  turquoise, deep turquoise,
  golden yellow, apricot nectar,
  candy pink, blush red, purple iris
Aleene's Tack-It adhesive
Accessories of choice: shirt, headband
Duncan Scribbles® iron-on transfer
  pencil
Tracing paper
Scissors
Heavy cardboard or shirt-painting
  board
Sewing needle
White sewing thread
Misting bottle filled with water
Masking tape

1. To make peach flower, tape fabric strip edges to cardboard pulling taut, but not stretching. Mist fabric with water until moist. Using color of choice, squeeze a line of shiny paint around fabric ⅛" from edge; paint color will run, forming a border as paint dries. Let dry. Turn fabric strip over and squeeze a line of matching iridescent paint around strip ⅛" from edge. Let dry. Trim fabric along outer edge of color border.

2. Sew two gathering threads, ⅛" apart, down center of fabric strip lengthwise. Pull threads to gather fabric and knot thread ends to secure. Fold fabric in half lengthwise and wrap in a spiral to form a rosette. Sew spirals in place using a needle and thread.

3. To make leaves, use transfer pencil and follow manufacturer's instructions to transfer patterns to fabric or paint outlines freehand. Follow flower strip instructions to paint each leaf and cut out along color border outline. Use needle and thread to tack desired number of leaves to bottom of each rosette.

4. Follow manufacturer's instructions to apply Tack-It adhesive to bottom of each flower and leaves cluster. Press clusters onto shirts, headbands, or other accessories.

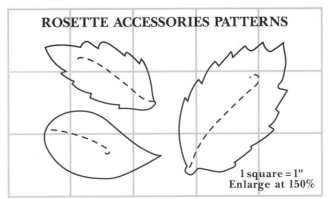

ROSETTE ACCESSORIES PATTERNS

1 square = 1"
Enlarge at 150%

Cool Cat & Hot Dog

For Ages: 3 yrs. and up

Materials (for **each** animal):
Two 12" squares black **or** tan Tempo foam-backed nylon fleece fabric or sweatshirt fleece fabric (for legs, tail, head, ears)
4" x 6" piece off-white Tempo foam-backed nylon fleece fabric or sweatshirt fleece (for muzzle)
7" square green **or** red Tempo foam-backed nylon fleece fabric or sweatshirt fleece (for bow)
Two ⅜" round buttons (for eyes)
¼" round or heart-shaped shank button (for nose)
Fairfield Processing polypropylene pellets
Polyester fiberfill
Threads to match fabrics
Quilting or upholstery thread
Disappearing-ink fabric-marking pen
Hot glue gun

Soft-sculpture needle	Pencil
Sewing machine	Point turner
Hand-sewing needle	Scissors
Tracing paper	Tape measure

1. Trace patterns onto tracing paper and cut out. Cut each piece from two layers of appropriate fabric with right sides facing . Use disappearing-ink fabric-marking pen to trace stitching line around pattern piece on wrong side of fabric, leaving at least ½" between pattern pieces; do not cut. Cut one 4½" x 1" strip of fabric for tail.

2. Sew both layers of each pattern piece together with right sides facing along outline. Cut out ¼" beyond seam line. Clip curves and points. Cut a slit in one side of each piece as indicated on patterns and in center of one muzzle piece. Turn, using point turner for cat's ears.

3. Mark and stitch topstitching lines at base of ears and down center of legs from toe to toe.

4. For tail, fold fabric strip in half lengthwise with right sides facing. Sew long edges together, using a ⅜" seam allowance. Turn. Turn under raw edges on one end of tail and whipstitch closed.

5. Stuff head and muzzle lightly with fiberfill. Slipstitch openings closed. Fill bottom three-fourths of leg channels with pellets and top fourth with fiberfill. Position raw end of tail in center of

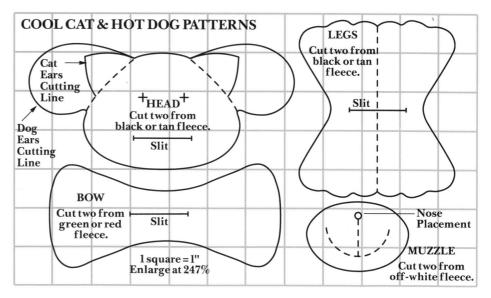

COOL CAT & HOT DOG PATTERNS

Cat Ears Cutting Line

Dog Ears Cutting Line

HEAD
Cut two from black or tan fleece.
Slit

BOW
Cut two from green or red fleece.
Slit

1 square = 1"
Enlarge at 247%

LEGS
Cut two from black or tan fleece.
Slit

Nose Placement

MUZZLE
Cut two from off-white fleece.

leg slit and slip stitch opening closed. Align head and leg slits with tail in back, and hand-sew head to legs.

6. Mark and stitch topstitching lines on muzzle. Sew button nose securely to muzzle with upholstery or quilting thread and soft-sculpture needle. Before cutting thread, take one stitch through center of mouth and pull tightly from behind to draw up and sculpt muzzle. Glue muzzle to face. Sew button eyes in place securely.

7. To make bow, fold bow piece in half lengthwise with slit on inside. Tie knot in center and pull out ends. Glue to dog's forehead or cat's chin.

Bunny Jump Rope & Baseball Card Box

Bunny Jump Rope

Abbreviations
beg—beginning
ch—chain(s)
hdc—half double crochet
rem—remaining
rnd(s)—round(s)
sc—single crochet
sl st—slip stitch
sk—skip
st(s)—stitch(es)

Materials:
1 oz. white worsted-weight yarn
Small amounts **each** pink and red
    worsted weight yarns
Size F aluminum crochet hook or size to
    obtain gauge
7' cotton clothesline rope
Two ½" blue pom-poms
Four ¼" pink pom-poms
Polyester fiberfill
White craft glue   Yarn needle

Gauge: 4 sc = 1"; 4 rnds sc = 1"
Finished size: Each bunny handle = 6"
long

1. Bunny (make two): Beg at top of head with white, ch 4; sl st in first ch to form a ring.
Rnd 1: Ch 1, work 9 sc in ring; sl st to beg ch-1—9 sts.
Rnd 2: Ch 1, sc in each st around; sl st to beg ch-1.
Rnd 3: Ch 1, 2 sc in each st around; sl st to beg ch-1—18 sts.
Rnds 4–9: Ch 1, sc in each st around; sl st to beg ch-1.
Rnd 10: Ch 1, (sk 1 st, sc in next st) around; sl st to beg ch-1—9 sts.
Rnds 11–15: Ch 1, sc in each st around; sl st to beg ch-1.
Rnd 16: Ch 1, sk 1 st, sc in each rem st around; sl st to beg ch-1.
Rnds 17–21: Ch 1, sc in each st around; sl st to beg ch-1. Fasten off after rnd 21. Referring to photo and using pink yarn, satin-stitch eyes and nose, and stemstitch mouth. Glue on pink pom-poms for cheeks.
2. Ears (make two for each bunny):
Rnd 1: With pink, ch 11, sc in 2nd ch from hook and sc in each ch across. Fasten off.
Rnd 2: Join white with sl st in first sc and in each st across, sc in end of strip, sc in each st on foundation ch. Fasten off. Sew ears to top of head.
3. Scarf (make two): With red, ch 16, hdc in 3rd ch from hook and in each ch across. Fasten off, leaving a tail of yarn.
4. Bow (make two): With red, ch 10, hdc in 3rd ch from hook and in each ch across. Fasten off. Sew a bow to the center front of each scarf. Glue a blue pom-pom to each bow center.
5. Finishing (for each bunny): Stuff head with fiberfill. Insert 3" of clothesline rope into bunny handle and stuff firmly around rope with fiberfill. Coat 2" of rope below bunny handle and 1" right side of handle with glue. Starting at bottom of glue on rope, tightly wind red yarn up around rope and handle; tuck yarn ends to inside and glue. Sew scarf around neck with bow centered in front.

Baseball Card Box

Materials:
5" x 7" x 3" wood box
DecoArt™ Americana™ True Colors
    acrylic paint, color: Prussian blue
DecoArt™ Americana™ gloss varnish
JHB buttons: five baseballs, three
    baseball gloves
1"-wide sponge paintbrush
Craft knife with sharp blade
Wire cutters   Tack cloth
Six baseball cards   Miniature bat
Thick craft glue   Fine sandpaper

1. Sand box lightly and wipe with tack cloth. Using sponge brush, paint with two coats of blue, letting dry between coats.
2. Glue baseball cards to top and sides of box, overlapping lid seam. When glue is dry, slit cards with craft knife along lid seam. Apply two coats of varnish to box, letting dry between coats.
3. Use wire cutters to cut shanks off buttons. Glue buttons and bat to box lid.

Kids' Fun Crafts

Let the children make cute stocking stuffers! Select projects suited to their ages, gather together the supplies they'll need, and watch your artistic geniuses at work! They may ask you to furnish milk and cookies, a very necessary "fuel" for inventive little crafters, but they will probably want to work at their own pace, without any (or much) help from the adults.

With the safe, easy, and fun crafts in this chapter, you can rest assured while the children stretch their ingenuity and make great presents for their friends, grandparents, and neighbors—maybe even their parents! Fashion accessories, eye-catching picture frames, and clever crafts with cookie cutters will tickle your youngsters' creative fancies.

Have a "Let's Craft party" for neighborhood children as well as your own. Select several projects, set up a work center for each complete with all the supplies needed, and get set to enjoy the role of "advisor" to your crafting group. For each child, decorate and label a brown bag to be used as a tote for carrying home his or her handiwork.

Cookie Cutter Crafts

For Ages: 3 yrs. and up

Materials:

Cookie cutters of choice

12" x 18" piece ½" Styrofoam® plastic foam sheet

Decorator and dimensional acrylic paint in colors of choice

Plain brown or white paper (for gift wrap)

Construction paper in colors of choice (for cards)

⅛"-wide ribbon in colors of choice (cut into 10" lengths, for hanging loops)

Multiloop ribbon bows in colors of choice

1 yd. rattail cord in color of choice (for necklace)

Beads or jewels of choice (for necklace and shirt)

Prewashed cotton blend shirt

Medium paintbrush

Florist's wire (cut into 1½" lengths, for hangers)

Aluminum foil

Scissors

Fabric glue

Thick craft glue

Paper towels

Sequins (optional)

Glitter (optional)

1. To cut out each shape, press cookie cutter firmly into foam sheet. Carefully remove shape from cutter.

2. Pour acrylic paint onto a piece of aluminum foil. Dip foam shape in paint to completely coat one side. Press shape onto surface of choice, making certain all edges touch surface. Lift shape, being careful not to smear paint. Repeat to stamp additional shapes, reloading with paint as necessary. If desired, sprinkle stamped shapes with glitter while paint is wet. To add writing or accent lines, let stamped shape dry completely, and then squeeze dimensional paint directly from the bottle.

3. To make cards and gift wrap, cut and fold construction paper to size of choice for each card, and cut plain paper to size for gift wrap. For an overall background effect, dip any foam shape in paint and dab excess on a paper towel. Stamp background repeatedly without reloading foam with paint. Let dry and follow Step 2 to stamp new shape and add writing and accent lines. Glue on sequins with craft glue if desired. For shirt, stamp with shapes and add jewels with fabric glue.

4. To make ornaments, let paint dry on each foam shape after stamping is completed. Paint opposite side and edges of shape to match. Add glitter or accent colors if desired. Bend florist's wire into a U shape, dip ends in glue, and insert in top edge of shape for a hanger. Thread one 10" ribbon length through hanger and knot ends or tie to multiloop bow.

5. To make necklace, thread rattail cord through hanger of completed ornament. String on beads and tie rattail ends together.

Fun Frames

For Ages: 8 yrs. and up

General Materials:
Two 5½" x 7" pieces and one 2" x 5"
    piece of heavy cardboard (for **each**
    frame)
Craft knife or scissors (use scissors for
    younger children)
Thick craft glue
Ruler
Tracing paper
Graphite paper
Pencil

Cat Frame
Materials:
Westrim® Fun Foam™: 5½" x 7" piece
    rose, 5" square purple, 1¼" circle
    lime, 2" x 3" piece yellow
Duncan Scribbles® 3-Dimensional
    Fabric Writers paint, colors:
    glittering amethyst, glittering ruby,
    glittering gold, iridescent golden
    green, shiny black, shiny white

1. Trace patterns onto tracing paper.
Use graphite paper and a sharp pencil
to lightly transfer cat pattern to purple
foam and bow pattern to yellow foam.
Use ruler to draw one 3" x 4½" rectangle each in center of rose foam and
center of one cardboard piece for
photo openings. Use craft knife or scissors to carefully cut out foam pieces
and each photo opening.
2. Refer to photo and squeeze paint directly from the bottle to add details.
Draw a curving line around rose foam
frame with green and add paw prints
with ruby. To paint cat, outline with
amethyst, add ears and nose with ruby,
and paint eyes with white; let dry, paint
pupils with black, and add remaining
facial features. Add a white highlight to
each eye when pupils are dry. Outline
bow with gold. With green, outline and
add detail lines to lime circle for yarn
ball. Let dry.
3. Glue rose foam frame over cardboard frame. Glue bow to cat's neck and
cat to bottom right corner of frame. Glue
ball to top left corner of frame.
4. To assemble frame, position photo
in opening and glue remaining 5"x 7"
cardboard piece to back. For stand, score

lightly across back of 2" x 5" cardboard strip, ½" down from top. Bend along score line and glue this ½" top of stand to center back of frame, 2½" from top edge.

Beach Frame
Materials:
Westrim® Fun Foam™: 5½" x 7" piece purple, 4" x 7" piece **each** rose and lime, 2" x 3" piece orange, 3" x 5" piece yellow
Duncan Scribbles® 3-Dimensional Fabric Writers paint, colors: glittering ruby, iridescent golden green, shiny bright yellow, shiny black

1. Follow *Cat Frame* directions to trace and transfer patterns and cut out photo openings. Cut frame from purple; tree trunk from rose; tree top from lime; seashell from orange; and sun, three beach ball segments, and starfish from yellow. Cut one 2" circle from orange for beach ball.
2. Refer to photo and squeeze paint directly from bottle to add details. Paint lines on the tree top and seashell with green, tree trunk with ruby, ball segments and starfish with yellow, and features on sun with black. Let paint dry.
3. Glue foam frame over cardboard frame. Glue sun to top right corner, orange beach ball to bottom right corner, and tree trunk to left side of frame, aligning bottom edges. Glue center of tree top only to frame at top of trunk. Glue shells to base of trunk and ball segments to beach ball.
4. Follow step 4 of *Cat Frame* directions to assemble frame.

Baseball Frame
Materials:
Westrim® Fun Foam™: 5½" x 7" piece lime, 3" square brown, 1" circle white, 3" x 3½" piece red, 2" square blue, 1½" x 6" piece tan
Duncan Scribbles® 3-Dimensional Fabric Writers paint, colors: iridescent copper, shiny bright red, shiny bright blue

1. Follow *Cat Frame* directions to trace and transfer patterns and cut out photo openings. Cut frame from lime, glove from brown, hat from blue, hat segment from red, and bat from tan. Glue hat segment to hat.
2. Refer to photo and squeeze paint directly from bottle to add details. Paint lines on glove and bat with copper, red hat segment and ball with red, and blue hat segments with blue. Glue hat segment

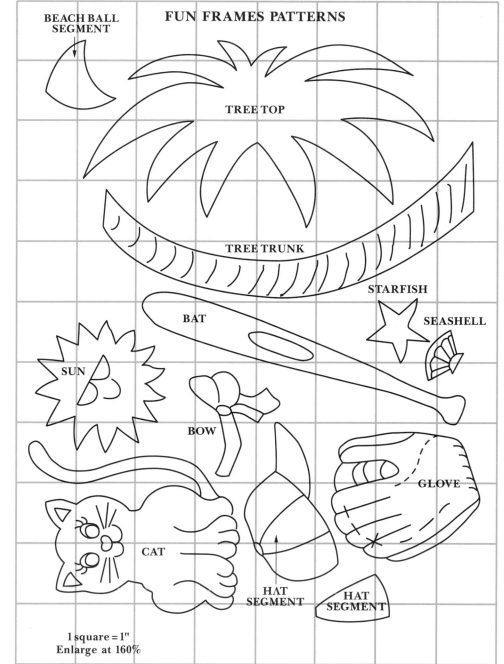

FUN FRAMES PATTERNS

BEACH BALL SEGMENT

TREE TOP

TREE TRUNK

STARFISH

BAT

SEASHELL

SUN

BOW

GLOVE

CAT

HAT SEGMENT

HAT SEGMENT

1 square = 1"
Enlarge at 160%

to hat and add outlines with blue and red paints.
3. Glue foam frame over cardboard frame. Glue glove to bottom left corner, hat to top left corner, and bat and then ball to bottom right corner. Paint year on left side of frame and "All Stars" across top.
4. Follow step 4 of *Cat Frame* directions to assemble frame.

Gifts for Friends

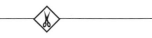

Friendship Doll Necklace

For Ages: 8 yrs. and up

Materials:
2½"-long wood clothespin (for **each** doll)
Pearl cotton in colors of choice
Fine-tip and wide-tip permanent black
    markers
Dark pink acrylic paint
Size 1 round paintbrush
1 yd. rattail cord in color of choice
Black seed beads (optional for buttons)
Thick craft glue   Toothpicks

1. Use fine-tip marker to draw eyes and mouth on head of each clothespin as shown in Pattern. Thin acrylic paint and paint cheeks on face. With wide-tip marker, add shoes to bottom of clothespin "legs."
2. To make a hanging loop for each doll, cut one 2" pearl cotton length and fold in half. Glue ends to center back of clothespin, aligning tops of loop and head.
3. Apply a thin layer of glue to clothespin from neck to ¾" from bottom edge for doll with dress, and to ½" from bottom for doll with pants. Referring to photo for clothing designs, begin at the neck and wrap lengths of pearl cotton around body, gluing down ends as you change colors. For skirt, wrap around both legs. Wrap around legs individually for pants. If desired, add decorative pearl cotton bows and belts, or glue on seed beads for buttons.
4. For arms on each doll, cut two 2½" lengths of pearl cotton. Tie ends together with an overhand knot. Glue center of strands to back and sides of body, bringing arms to front.
5. For straight hair styles, cut pearl cotton to length desired and glue to head, being careful not to cover hanging loop. For braided style, braid three pearl cotton strands together and use a contrasting color to wrap ends. Glue to top and sides of head. For curly hair, wrap wet pearl cotton around a toothpick, and let dry. Remove from toothpick, cut into lengths of choice, and glue to head.
6. String hanging loops onto rattail cord, knotting cord around each loop. Trim cord ends to desired length and knot together.

Fantastic Pens

For Ages: 8 yrs. and up

Materials:
Aleene's Fantastic Plastic™ Modeling
    Plastic, three colors of choice
Pen refill cartridges
1½"- to 2"-diameter cookie cutters in
    shapes of choice
Smooth work surface
Scrap of cotton fabric
Liquid dishwashing soap
Electric frying pan
Waxed paper
Toothpick   Fork

Note: Adult supervision is suggested for younger children.

1. Fill frying pan with 1" of water and heat to 120°, or near boiling. Maintain water level and temperature while working for best results. Place each cookie cutter on a square of waxed paper.
2. Measure one capful of each modeling plastic color and pour into hot water. Pellets should begin to melt together immediately. (**Note:** If pellets float, water temperature is too cool.) Use a fork to remove melted pellets from water. Working quickly, blot excess water on fabric scrap and roll each color between hand to form a rope. Roll and twist three colors together into a long, smooth rope, approximately ¼" in diameter. (**Note:** If plastic begins to harden, use fork to dip rope in and out of hot water to soften. Blot water and continue.) Beginning and ending at bottom of cookie cutter shape, wrap plastic rope around outside of cookie cutter. Let cool and remove plastic from cookie cutter.
3. To cover pen, repeat step 2 to melt three colors of plastic and form rope. Beginning at top of pen refill cartridge, wrap plastic rope around cartridge and roll on a smooth surface until smooth and even. Pinch off excess plastic at ends, exposing writing tip at one end and ink cartridge hole at the other end. Dip bottom of plastic cookie cutter shape and top of pen in and out of hot water quickly to soften. Press shape to top of pen, smoothing plastic with fingers, and leaving a small opening in the plastic over ink cartridge end. (**Note:** The pen will not write if ink cartridge end is covered.) If necessary, soften pen top in hot water and make an air hole over cartridge with a toothpick.
4. Clean pan with warm soapy water.

Vinyl Covered Bookmarks

For Ages: 3 yrs. and up

Materials:
Construction paper in colors of choice
12" length yarn or narrow ribbon in
    color of choice (for **each** bookmark)
Clear self-adhesive vinyl
Assorted paper cutouts, stamps, stickers
Fine-tip permanent markers in colors
    of choice (for shaped bookmarks)
Paper punch   White craft glue
Scissors   Pencil
Tracing paper   Graphite paper

1. For **each** rectangular bookmark, cut one 1¾" x 6" piece from construction paper. Glue on paper cutouts, stamps, or stickers.
2. For **each** shaped bookmark, trace pattern and cut out. Use graphite paper to transfer pattern lightly to construction paper. Cut out shape and use markers to add details. Glue to contrasting color paper and cut out ¼" beyond shape.
3. To finish **each** bookmark, cut two pieces of clear self-adhesive vinyl, ½" larger than the construction paper. Remove backing and adhere to both sides of construction paper. Leaving a ¼" border all around, trim excess vinyl. Punch hole in center top of each bookmark and thread ribbon through hole, knotting close to top of bookmark.

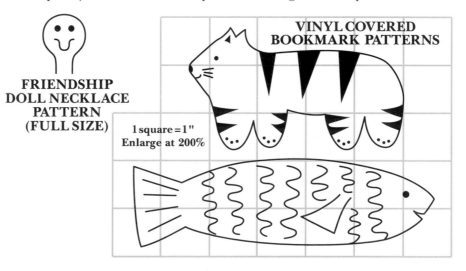

FRIENDSHIP DOLL NECKLACE PATTERN (FULL SIZE)

VINYL COVERED BOOKMARK PATTERNS

1 square = 1"
Enlarge at 200%

Santa Claus &
Cheerleader Ties

Santa Claus Tie

For Ages: 10 yrs. and up

Materials:
Black necktie
Felt scraps: red, beige, white
One & Only Creations white Mini
 Curl™ Curly Hair™
¾" x 2½" strip white acrylic fur
12-mm gold jingle bell
¼" red pom-pom
Two 10-mm wiggle eyes
6" length ⅛"-wide green satin ribbon,
 tied into bow
Duncan Scribbles® 3-Dimensional
 Fabric Writers paint, color:
 white iridescent
Small amount of polyester fiberfill
Black & Decker® 2 Temp™ glue gun
Tracing paper
Pencil   Scissors

1. Trace patterns onto tracing paper
and cut out. Cut pieces from felt as indicated on patterns. Cut one 2¼" circle
from beige felt for head.
2. For face, place a small amount of
fiberfill behind head and position head
4" up from bottom of tie. With glue gun
set on low, glue edges of head to tie.
3. Fold under ¼" on side edges of hat as
indicated by dotted lines on pattern. Position hat with ¾" overlapping head top,
stuff under hat lightly with fiberfill,
and glue hat edges to tie and head. Cut
off corners of acrylic fur strip to make
round and glue strip to base of hat. Glue
jingle bell to top of hat and green bow
to one side.
4. Refer to photo and glue hair across
forehead, to sides of face, and to chin
for beard. Glue eyes, mustache, and
pom-pom nose to face.
5. Using white paint, add snowflakes
to tie. For each snowflake, squeeze
paint directly from bottle to make an X.
Paint a plus sign over the X, aligning
centers. Squeeze small dots around
each snowflake.

Cheerleader Tie

For Ages: 10 yrs. and up

Materials:
Blue necktie
Felt scraps: red, beige, white, pink
One & Only Creations blonde Mini
 Curl™ Curly Hair™
Two 1" red pom-poms

2" length 1"-wide red satin box-pleated
 ribbon (for skirt)
Duncan Scribbles® 3-Dimensional
 Fabric Writers paint, colors: navy
 blue, glittering gold
Fine-tip permanent black marker
Small amount polyester fiberfill
Black & Decker 2 Temp™ glue gun
Paper punch with ¼" hole
Waxed paper
Scissors
Tracing paper   Pencil

1. Trace patterns onto tracing paper and
cut out. Cut pieces from felt as indicated
on patterns. Cut one ⅞" circle from beige
felt for head and two ⅜" white felt
squares for socks. Use paper punch to
punch two pink felt circles for cheeks.
2. With glun gun set on low, glue legs
to tie, 3" up from point. Aligning

edges, glue shorts over leg tops and
glue socks and then shoes to bottoms
of legs. Position sweater with bottom
edge touching top of legs, stuff a small
amount of fiberfill under tummy area,
and glue sweater edges to tie. Glue
head at top of sweater, slightly overlapping sweater edge.
3. Referring to photo for details, glue
cheeks to head, and then use the marker
to add facial features. Glue hair to top
and sides of head. Glue one pom-pom
to end of each arm. Turn under and
glue short ends of pleated ribbon and
then bound edge to the waistline.
4. Using paint directly from bottle,
squeeze ½"-high navy blue school letters of choice onto waxed paper and let
dry. Peel off and glue to sweater. Use
glittering gold paint to add lines and
stars to tie.

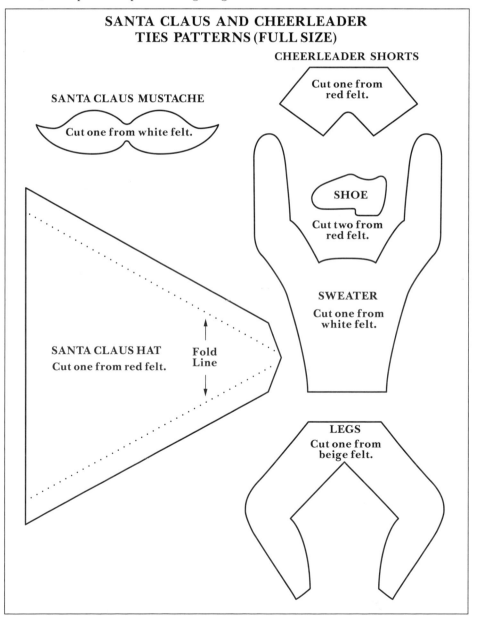

**SANTA CLAUS AND CHEERLEADER
TIES PATTERNS (FULL SIZE)**

CHEERLEADER SHORTS

Cut one from
red felt.

SANTA CLAUS MUSTACHE

Cut one from white felt.

SHOE

Cut two from
red felt.

SWEATER
Cut one from
white felt.

SANTA CLAUS HAT
Cut one from red felt.

Fold
Line

LEGS
Cut one from
beige felt.

Puzzle Piece Accessories

For Ages: 5 yrs. and up

Materials:
Jigsaw puzzle pieces
Accessories: visors, button covers,
   barrettes, hair combs
Duncan Decorator Acrylic Paint in
   colors of choice
Duncan Hi-Gloss Sealer
Paintbrushes, sizes: medium flat, 1 liner
Thick craft glue

1. Use flat brush to base-coat puzzle
pieces, painting both sides and edges,
with color of choice. Let dry. Use liner
brush to add stripes, squiggles, dots,
checks, or outlines with contrasting colors. Let dry.
2. Apply a coat of sealer to front and
edges of painted pieces and let dry.
3. Glue pieces to accessories in single or
stacked layers as desired.

Giant Yo-Yo

For Ages: 10 yrs. and up

Note: Adult assistance required for drilling hole.

Materials for **each** yo-yo:
Two empty plastic 32 oz. soda bottles with flat-ridged bottoms
DecoArt™ Liquid Sequins™ glitter paint, colors: Blue Twinkle **or** Brilliant Burgundy
1"-wide soft paintbrush
Two 25-mm round acrylic mirrors to match paint color
40" length Kreinik #32 metallic braid in matching color
Blair® deco art glazer
¼" x ¾" bolt with nut
Two ³/₁₆" washers
Craft cutters or scissors
Drill with ¼" bit

1. For each yo-yo half, cut off plastic bottle bottom ½" above bottom ridge. Trim plastic evenly along ridge. Drill a hole with ¼" bit in center of bottle bottom.
2. Paint both sides and edges of each yo-yo half with several even coats of paint, letting dry between coats. Spray with art glazer and let dry.
3. To assemble yo-yo, slide one washer, one yo-yo half with cut edge up, and another washer onto bolt. Tie one end of metallic braid loosely around bolt. Slide remaining yo-yo half with cut edge down, remaining washer, and nut onto bolt. Tighten nut slightly, make certain braid is centered when yo-yo is in a hanging position, and then tighten nut securely.
4. Glue acrylic mirror to center of each yo-yo half, covering nut and bolt. Tie a 2" loop in end of metallic braid.

Colorful Creations

Painted Tile Trivets

For Ages: 3 yrs. and up

Note: Adult assistance required for using oven.

Materials:
6" to 8" white ceramic tile squares
Self-adhesive felt square to fit back of **each** tile square
Liquitex® Glossies™ Acrylic Enamels in colors of choice
Paintbrushes: medium flat and liner
Oven
Pencil

1. For handprint tile, trace around child's hand on front of tile with pencil. Paint hand with color of choice and let dry. Paint name and date or desired message on hand and add decorative border around tile. Paint edges to coordinate with handprint color.
2. For artwork and Christmas tree tiles, draw design on front of tile with pencil. Paint design, letting paint dry before painting another color on top. Paint edges with coordinating color.
3. Follow paint manufacturer's directions to bake tiles. Baked tiles will be heat-proof. Let tiles cool, and adhere felt to back.

Decorated Soaps

For Ages: 3 yrs. and up

Materials:
Scented soaps in assorted shapes and sizes
Assorted cotton fabric scraps (stripes, dots, checks, etc.)
Scraps of ribbon, lace, yarn
Trims: jingle bells, small silk flowers, large buttons, pom-poms
Pinking shears
Scissors
White craft glue

1. Unwrap soaps and discard paper wrappers.
2. Using pinking shears, cut fabric pieces at least 1" larger than needed to wrap around soaps. Wrap fabric neatly around each soap, overlapping and gluing fabric edges. **Note:** Do not glue fabric to soap.
3. Refer to photo for trim placement. Wrap and glue ribbon, lace, or yarn around soap. Glue on trims of choice.

Quilt Block Photo Ornaments

For Ages: 5 yrs. and up

Materials for each ornament:
4½"-square ½" Styrofoam® plastic foam sheet
Christmas calicos or solid color fabrics of choice (cut into one 5" square for back and eight 2" squares)
Photograph, trimmed to 1½" square
20" length ⅛"-wide trim or braid of choice (cut into 5" lengths)
18½" length ⅜"-wide grosgrain ribbon in coordinating color
8" length ⅛"-wide satin ribbon to match grosgrain ribbon
Four 5-mm gold beads
½" long sequin pins
Aleene's Tacky glue
Fine-tip permanent black marker
Ruler
Sharp pencil
Scissors
¾"-1½" putty knife

1. Use ruler and permanent marker to divide one side of foam sheet square into nine 1½" squares. Score lines using ruler and sharp pencil.

2. For front, begin in one corner of foam square and center one 2" fabric square over marked square on foam sheet. Holding putty knife perpendicular to surface, use knife to press fabric edges into foam along scored lines. Repeat to cover all eight outside squares, leaving center square uncovered. Glue excess fabric to side edges of foam, trimming fabric as necessary to lay smooth. Center fabric backing square over foam square back and glue fabric to side edges of foam. Glue photo to center square.

3. Glue 5" trim lengths over seam lines. Glue grosgrain ribbon around foam edges, covering fabric edges and trim ends. Make a loop with satin ribbon and knot 1" from ends. Glue ribbon ends to top corner of ornament.

4. Thread four gold beads onto sequin pins. Dip pin ends in glue and insert in ornament at photo corners.

Stitch Illustrations

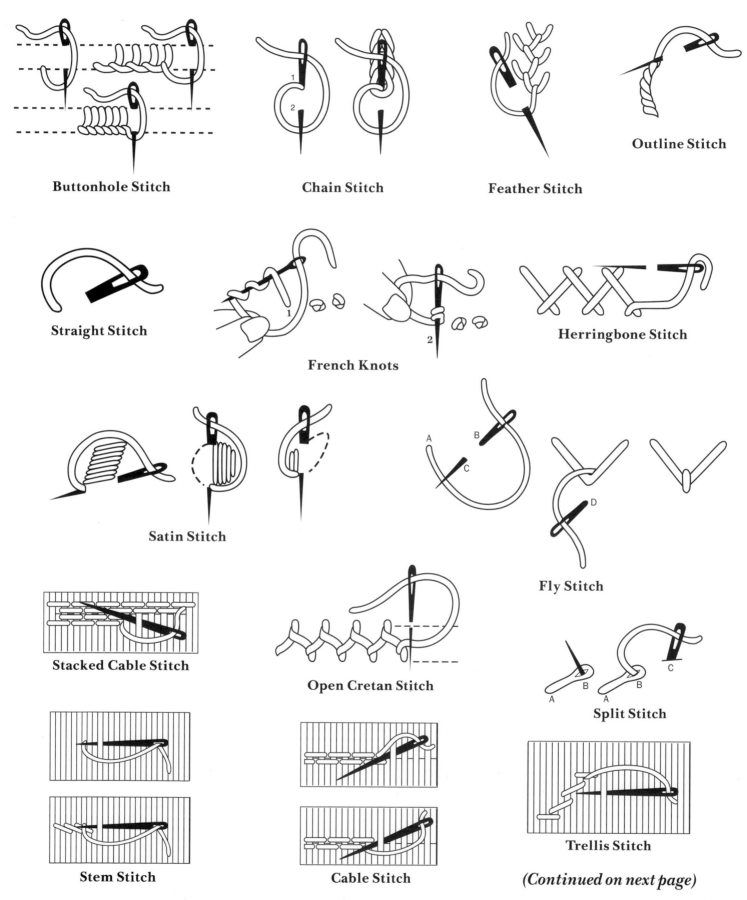

Buttonhole Stitch

Chain Stitch

Feather Stitch

Outline Stitch

Straight Stitch

French Knots

Herringbone Stitch

Satin Stitch

Fly Stitch

Stacked Cable Stitch

Open Cretan Stitch

Split Stitch

Stem Stitch

Cable Stitch

Trellis Stitch

(Continued on next page)

141

Stitch Illustrations (cont.)

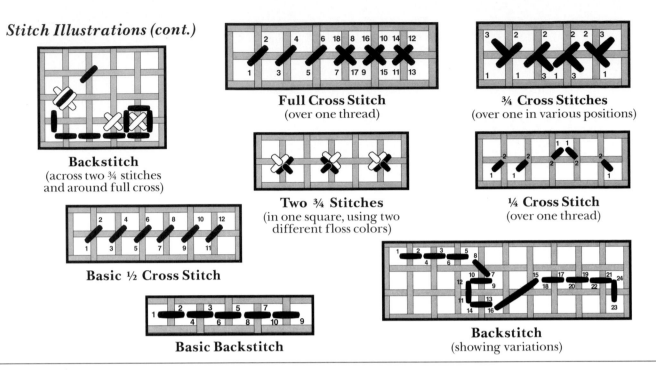

Backstitch
(across two ¾ stitches
and around full cross)

Full Cross Stitch
(over one thread)

¾ Cross Stitches
(over one in various positions)

Basic ½ Cross Stitch

Two ¾ Stitches
(in one square, using two
different floss colors)

¼ Cross Stitch
(over one thread)

Basic Backstitch

Backstitch
(showing variations)

Shopper's Guide

Back Street Designs, 100 East Washington Street, Post Office Box 1213, Athens, AL 35611.

Bagworks Inc., 3933 California Parkway East, Fort Worth, TX 76119-7346.

Birdhouse Enterprises, 110 Jennings Avenue, Patchogue, NY 11772. To order a set of seven Christmas charms for $7 and/or 15" x 18" tan fabric for $3.50, send total amount plus $3 shipping and handling. NY residents add 8½% sales tax.

Black & Decker Inc., c/o Craft Marketing Connections, 2363 460th Street, Ireton, IA 51027.

Capitol Imports Inc., Box 13002, Tallahassee, FL 32317.

Charles Craft, Inc., Box 1049, Laurinburg, NC 28353.

Crafter's Pride from Daniel Enterprises, Box 1105, Laurinburg, NC 28353.

Creative Beginnings, 375 Morro Bay Boulevard, Morro Bay, CA 93442.

DecoArt, Post Office Box 360, Stanford, KY 40484.

The DMC Corporation, order from Craft Gallery, Ltd., Post Office Box 145, Swampscott, MA 01907.

Duncan Enterprises, 5673 East Shields Avenue, Fresno, CA 93727.

Eberhard Faber products, distributed by American Art Clay Co. Inc., 4717 West 16th Street, Indianapolis, IN 46222.

Fairfield Processing Corp., Post Office Drawer 1157, Danbury, CT 06813.

Faultless Starch/Bon Ami, 1025 West 8th Street, Kansas City, MO 64101-1200.

Home Crafted Toys™, Stitcher's Kaleidoscope from Homecrafters Manufacturing Corp., 1859 Kenion Point, Snellville, GA 30278.

JHB International Inc., 1955 South Quince Street, Denver, CO 80231.

Kreinik threads and braids available from The Daisy Chain, Post Office Box 1258, Parkersburg, WV 26102.

MPR Associates, Post Office Box 7343, High Point, NC 27264.

One & Only Creations, 210 Ornduff Street, Box 2730, Napa, CA 94558.

Styrofoam® brand products from The Dow Chemical Company, 2020 Dow Center, Midland, MI 48674.

Tempo® fabric, send a SASE to Lynne Farris Designs, 629 Cherokee Avenue, Atlanta, GA 30312 for ordering information.

St. Louis Trimming, Inc., 5040 Arsenal Street, Saint Louis, MO 63139.

Sudberry House, Colton Road, Box 895, Old Lyme, CT 06371.

Westrim®, available at craft and chain stores.

Wright's, South Street, West Warren, MA 01092-0398.

Zim's Inc., 4370 South 300 West, Box 7620, Salt Lake City, UT 84107.

Designer Credits

Georgia Ball, *Embroidered Hearts,* page 30; *Embroidered Fingertip Towel,* page 64; *Whimsical Menagerie,* page 118.

Sandy Belt, *Annie Apple Doll,* page 38; *Victorian Pig & Bunny Dolls,* page 102.

Gail Bird and Cheryl Mihills, *"Charming" Christmas Tree,* page 75.

Mary Polityka Bush for Kreinik Manufacturing, *Watch Pincushion,* page 42.

Maureen Carlson, *Angelic Trio,* page 82.

Sandy Cobb for Faultless Starch/Bon Ami, *Grandma's Treasure Bag,* page 40.

Elinor Czarnecki, *Sewing Caddy,* page 46.

Phyllis Dunstan, *Friendship Doll Necklace,* page 132.

Sandy Dye, *Sunflower Table Toppers,* page 62.

Dorothy Egan, *Watermelon Mugs & Flowerpots,* page 52.

Betty Davis Ernst for Duncan Enterprises, *Trellis Lunch Bag,* page 40.

Cheryl Fall, *Happy Cook Pot Holder,* page 55.

Lynne Farris, *Baby Dinosaur Puppets,* page 106; *I-Can-Dress-Myself Busy Book,* page 116; *Cool Cat & Hot Dog,* page 124.

Maria Filosa for The Dow Chemical Company, *Cookie Cutter Crafts,* page 128.

Wayne Fox and Vivian Peritts, *Giant Yo-Yo,* page 137.

Barbara Guyette, *Molded Soaps,* page 64.

Jennifer Haasl for Duncan Enterprises, *Gingerbread Stocking,* page 26; *Ornament Stocking,* page 27; *Puzzle Piece Accessories,* page 136.

Cindy Groom Harry, *Santa Claus & Cheerleader Ties,* page 134.

Diane Herbot, *Crazy-Quilt Box,* page 58.

Nancy Hoerner, *Santa Kaleidoscope,* page 80.

Charlotte Cathey Holder, *Kitten & Puppy Stockings,* page 10; *Christmas Afternoon Stocking,* page 18; *Teacher's Eraser,* page 44; *Cross-Stitch Towels,* page 56; *Carousel Cup* and *Bib,* page 110.

Pam Houk, *Stockings for Pets,* page 11; *Jar Lid Covers,* page 42; *Watermelon Apron,* page 52; *Button Box,* page 58; *Strip-Quilted Mitt & Towel,* page 60; *Angel Wall Hanging,* page 72; *Button Cross-Stitch Ornaments,* page 78; *Autograph Dog,* page 120; *Baseball Card Box,* page 125.

Marilyn Howard, *Smocked Sunglasses Case,* page 109.

Nancy Jolemore for The DMC Corporation, *Ethnic Bracelets,* page 94.

KD Artistry (Diane Davis, Kathy Wirth), *Vinyl Teddy Bear Toy,* page 110.

Annabelle Keller, *Yo-Yo Mini-Totes,* page 85.

Annabelle Keller for The Dow Chemical Company, *Party Favor Baskets,* page 84; *Windowsill Trees,* page 81; *Quilt Block Photo Ornaments,* page 140.

Connie Matricardi, *Easy Appliqué Purse,* page 90; *Vinyl Covered Bookmarks,* page 132; *Decorated Soaps,* page 138.

Linda McCoy, *Santa Table Set,* page 68.

Donna M. McCullough, *Silk Tie Business Cardholder,* page 98.

Liz Miller, *Purse Organizers,* page 88.

Vivian Peritts, *Clown Scissors Keeper,* page 37; *Fabric-Covered Belt & Earrings,* page 90; *Apple & Watermelon Coin Purses,* page 96; *Spot the Dog,* page 121.

Jan Powers, *Catnip Mouse,* page 34; *Stenciled Sachet Bag,* page 40.

Fran Queen for MPR Associates, *Satin Ribbon Clown,* page 105.

Hélène Rush, *Crochet & Knit Stockings,* page 15; *Golf Club Covers,* page 45; *Garden Wall Quilt,* page 59.

Judith Sandstrom, *Quilted Star Book Cover & Star Mini-Quilt,* page 32.

Ruth G. Shepherd, *Bunny Jump Rope,* page 125.

Margaret Sindelar, *Victorian Patchwork Stocking,* page 8; *Christmas Afternoon Stocking* finishing, page 18; *Yo-Yo Stocking,* page 24; *Dog* and *Cat Quilts,* page 34; *Teacher's Eraser* finishing, page 44; *Musical Note & Angel Book marks,* page 48; *Mother's Memory Book,* page 49; *Eyeglasses Cases,* page 98.

Jonica Starr for Duncan Enterprises, *Painted Socks,* page 115; *Rosette Accessories,* page 123; *Puzzle Piece Accessories,* page 136.

Dee Dee Triplett, *Stocking Pin,* page 71; *Cherry Pincushion & Pin,* page 92; *Necklace for All Seasons,* page 94.

Valerie Ward for Duncan Enterprises, *Painted Sneakers,* page 114.

Marianne Wourms for The DMC Corporation, *Kitchen Magnets,* page 54.

Carol Zentgraf, *Painted Nutcrackers,* page 76; *Fun Frames,* page 130; *Fantastic Pens,* page 132.

Carolyn Zentgraf, *Colorful Creations,* page 138.

Index

Numbers in **bold** type indicate color photo pages. All other numbers refer to pages for charts, color codes, patterns, and instructions.